AMERICAN SUCCESS PATHWAYS

By JANET RANGI

ISBN: 978-0-578-55519-5

This book is dedicated to my late dad for his selfless acts of kindness and humility.

License Notes

Thank you for respecting the hard work of this author.

TABLE OF CONTENTS

INTRODUCTION

America has long been viewed as the land where dreams can come true. This is according to a survey on immigration conducted by Public Agenda in 2009. America is made up of immigrants and remains the land of opportunity for many around the world. In fact, many people from all over the world dream and desire to move to the United States. Fueled by many desires like adventure, economic, political and religious reasons, this hope has not diminished over the years. This is proved by the fact that immigrants of the past are not different from the immigrants of today. However, studies have shown that recent immigrants also known to some as New Americans are entering the United States with higher education levels compared to previous immigrants. They are all bound by one goal of getting the opportunity to see their dreams fulfilled. America is a representation of every religion and race, and yet, the country is not defined by these things. Rather, the United States is viewed as a beacon of hope and freedom to people all over the world.

My name is Janet Rangi, and I was raised in Kenya. I came to the United States in 2003 as a student with 200 dollars in my pocket. I chose to be a VICTOR and not a VICTIM of my circumstances. I am an American citizen by naturalization. I have made a life and a career in the United States and I am part of what some would arguably call the American dream. The desire for economic emancipation and career progression was fulfilled and even perhaps exceeded in this journey.

What started as a desire and a dream has become a reality, and in the following few chapters, I will try, and share snippets based on personal experience as a new American. Hopefully, you will learn a thing or two on how to make decisions before and after coming to America. Through the course of the book, you will read through the lessons I have learnt, the mistakes I have made and wisdom that I have gathered over the years. I do this in the hope that perhaps through my journey, you will draw your inspiration to dream and fulfil your inspirations and desires. This book will not only serve as an inspiration for one who wants to come to the United States in pursuit of a better life but for anyone who desires to see their dream come true in any part of the world. I am a testament that dreams do come true and that all dreams are valid. In a nutshell, I will cut your learning curve. In my mind, I believed there was something bigger than what is my reality.

This niggling feeling is what birthed my desire to migrate to the United States; I heard about foreign nurses who were moving to the United States, and this desire was born out of wanting a better future. Through my successful transition, I managed to assist others to also immigrate through this process. I have guided them into very lucrative, successful money-making careers and jobs. Through this process, I garnered the credibility, the knowledge and experience required to write this book.

In this book, I explain the process of making decisions and how I navigated through the various hurdles. Getting here was not an easy process and I feel that I need to help those aspiring to become new Americans to take the same step with a few tips on how to make this dream come true. The process does not begin with getting here but with the purpose of coming and application of the right visa. After getting here there is settling in, adapting to the different culture and systems, and lastly getting the right immigration papers to make the stay permanent. I will give more detailed information about jobs, especially in the health care industry and the potential of making lots of money in the millions of dollars over time just by making good decisions. Through this book, I will give advice and share through my own personal experiences and the experiences of others who have been through a similar process. I do hope that you enjoy the book as much as I enjoyed writing it.

WHO IS JANET RANGI?

A fter graduating from the University of Eastern Africa, Baraton, I managed to move to the United States permanently and became a United States Citizen.

I am a graduate of the University of California, Los Angeles where I completed my Master's Degree in Family Nurse Practice. I also completed my postgraduate studies from the University of Texas Rio Grande Valley, where I specialized in Psychiatry and Mental health.

My passion for helping people started when I graduated and was jobless. I remember the pressure of trying hard to have a decent lifestyle. Eventually, I got a job, but the job could barely pay my bills.

My dream of coming to America changed my life forever. Having stayed in the United States close to 16 years, I have amassed a wealth of knowledge and experience. I have never forgotten where I came from and therefore, I have a passion for giving back to the people in my community.

I found a passion in blogging and Vlogging. This is evident from the hundreds of videos I made and articles I have written that have allowed me to interact with countless of followers in order to solve their problems.

I have spent hundreds if not thousands of hours digging valuable information and responding to thousands of questions. This has allowed me to garner a wealth of information that eventually, I decided to package into a book. "The American Success Pathways ".

That is why I want to provide a different pathway to success, especially those wishing to change their lives for the better. I hope to inspire those who follow my work to start thinking outside the box in a world that seems to have limited opportunities. From personal experience, the world is full of abundance.

I managed to grab some of these opportunities available and therefore, I have a responsibility to share with my community some of the tips and avenues that can lead to success specifically for those who believe in themselves.

Although nothing is promised, those who put in practice what I deliver through my regular blogs and books are more likely to succeed. We all need to search in the right places. I always say in my blogs that we need to know what the world knows because information is power.

Kindly note that I am not an immigration lawyer and by no means do I provide legal advice or attempt to file immigration benefits. However, I do provide true and tested information based on my personal and professional experience in the United States.

I have talked about so many ways of coming to America. You must know which ones are going to help you and the ones that fit you best. For starters, visit the US Department of State to learn more about visa categories. Learn the differences between Immigrant and Non-immigrant visas. Immigrant visas are also referred to as green cards, which simply means becoming a United States permanent resident. Non-immigrant visas are temporary in nature with the expectation of coming to America temporarily and returning to your home country.

REAL TESTIMONIALS

❝ *Hello Janet, my wife and I have been watching you and to God be the glory we tried again by attacking the elephant in the room. And we GOT IT JANET; we are picking our passports on Tuesday Janet!!!! I am a Film Maker and a YouTube Ambassador; I need to come on your show when I come to America Janet. God bless YOU....Keep up the good work Janet!!!!"*

"Hello Janet, I want to appreciate you and your advice. I got my B1/B2 visa last week Thursday. I'm coming back to the US and will open doors for my daughter now, learning so much valuable information from your videos. Thank you so much, hope I meet you and do a video together with you!"

"Hello Janet, been watching your videos and went to the embassy prepared got the visa been to Orlando for conference, it's been awesome thank you greatly"

"Hi Janet. Yesterday I was at the US Embassy Nairobi and I got the visa (B1B2). Travelling in April. Thank you very much dear for the encouragement. I Have not been following you every day. I have learnt a lot from you and am very grateful God Bless you so much"

Real Reviews

Very Authentic Information and passionate to help.

She is very good. She is a good source of information.

I can imagine how hard she has to work to give us all this information when still she is balancing with her life....I just met her today, but I can say this is so impressive...she is very selfless ready to share with everybody about green cards, scholarships, students visas and all that ...keep up Janet. I just love how you keep up the good work. You are a true Leader.

Very resourceful, informative, motivational, and very generous with information.

Information is indeed key. so, keep researching and digging deep to be fully informed

Full of motivation, encouragement and intelligence, a teacher, a director and a blogger, I love her so much and I hope to meet with her someday.

The most inspiring lady you will EVER come across. Full of wisdom and honesty in everything!!!

Truly I can't explain how wonderful this loving is; it is just like a miracle when more people have succeeded through this. Guys wake up and decide. Anyway, more thanks to this director and God bless you for your effort of trying to help the less privileged, keep it up.

Wisdom. Janet is full of wisdom and kindhearted. At least she isn't mean with information. I thank God for Janet Rangi.

No hard work, no gain. You are right Janet. No one offers great advice like you do free of charge my sister. May God bless you. Friends follow and listen to Janet, but most important act upon what she says and continue to have the desire to succeed.

The idea of Janet Rangi brand is worth to utilize. The period of its launch has power to have information, power to help myself and many others to carry out effective research on various global issues. moving forward Janet get yourself to equip us with health and wellness information as its exploiting our resources just like employment, poverty and education. Otherwise praying that God should empower you with health, wellness and needed resources as you continue sharing all you are doing to help the universe. Be blessed.

UNDERSTANDING HOW JANET CAME TO THE UNITED STATES

...using nursing as a pathway to a green card and eventually getting the American citizenship.

W e must talk about nursing as one of the pathways to obtain green cards and eventually becoming American citizens. So, our topic today is NURSING. Speaking of something I know because I came to the United States with a bachelor's degree in nursing. I graduated from the University of Eastern Africa Baraton school of Nursing. After graduation, I completed a mandatory one-year internship at Kenyatta National Hospital, at which time I sat for the Nursing Council examinations. I was finally registered as a community health nurse in the Republic of Kenya. After the internship, I was lucky to find a job at the Aga Khan Hospital Nairobi, where I worked as a registered nurse in a male surgical ward.

I was generally that kind of a person who kept my ears open for any new opportunities. Even with the high unemployment rates back home, I still had my dreams. I was going to make it regardless. I was burning for change. I had a STRONG DESIRE TO SUCCEED. Going to America would offer me a chance to change my life. I would see doctors and pharmacists driving to the hospital in private cars, but as a registered nurse, I could not afford that. I took public transportation. I knew one day I would finally drive my own car. That was my motivation.

Let us focus on what led to my achievements. Eventually, I met foreign nursing agents in Nairobi. No names here because those nursing agents are no longer in the same business. However, keep reading because I will provide examples of nursing agents if you are interested in working as a registered nurse in the United States. They helped me to apply for a nursing job in the United States. At that time, I did not understand what was going on, but importantly, I listened and followed directions. I was instructed to provide documents such as my nursing transcripts, graduation certificates and my nursing license. I did exactly that.

On the day, to my surprise, I received a phone call from the United States. The human resource manager from a hospital in New Jersey was on the line. She introduced herself and explained the reason for her call. She was about to interview me for a nursing job in the United States. She asked about my job experiences. I explained more about medical surgical nursing because that was my main experience.

In conclusion, she asked if I loved to work in a big city or a smaller community hospital. I was so excited because for me it did not matter. I wanted to come to America. "the land of milk and honey". Several days went by before she offered me a nursing job. She offered 21 dollars per hour. I was so excited that I did not care how much they paid me. I wanted to cross the oceans. I shared the news with my parents. My dad was so happy and proud of her daughter. He mentioned that the cost of living was expensive in the United States. Again, I did not care so long as I had a job in the United States. Meanwhile, I moved on with my life and got married to a dentist. Eventually, I was pregnant with my son.

One day in the evening, I received a phone call from one of my friends. He was a Registered Nurse at Nairobi Hospital in Kenya. We had received envelopes from a sponsor in the United States. I know sponsor means many things. No relationship strings with the sponsor; it was pure business. We had been admitted at St Michaels College in Vermont to study English as a Second Language for 6 months. The American sponsor was to pay for all expenses including tuition, food and housing.

How lucky! At this point, I became worried about my situation because I was newly married and pregnant. This was going to be a very difficult decision. Anyway, I booked an appointment for an F-1 Student visa at the American embassy in Nairobi. To cut a long story short, I was lucky to get that Visa, the rest were denied. I departed for the United States in August 2003 with 200 dollars in my pocket.

After arriving at St Michaels college in Vermont, I met Registered Nurses from the Philippines. They were preparing for nursing examinations, also known as NCLEX. This exam is done by all registered nurses in the United States. I attended the English classes at St Michaels college, but in my mind, I knew the clock was ticking with my pregnancy. I was 8 months pregnant. I called my American sponsor because I wanted to register for the NCLEX. I was worried about giving birth before passing the NCLEX. My sponsor was very reluctant to register me for the exam. In his opinion, the exam was very difficult without adequate preparation. In fact, many foreign nurses were failing the NCLEX.

Remember I wrote earlier that I was following directions anytime my nursing agent told me to send my documents to the United States? Luckily, all my documents had been received by the Commission on Graduates of Foreign Nursing Schools popularly known as CGFNS. The same documents had been received by the Nevada Board of Nursing. In that case, I already had permission to test for the NCLEX. I will write more information in detail because this is the process of getting licensed as a registered nurse in the United States.

Moving on regarding exam registration, the sponsor recommended at least 6 months of exam preparation. He was not aware of my pregnancy. I did not want to tell him anything about my pregnancy before leaving Kenya because I knew this was a life changing opportunity. I was not going to reveal anything that would jeopardize my chances of going to America. I insisted on taking the NCLEX as soon as possible. My sponsor eventually gave in and registered me for the exam before I gave birth to my son.

I was officially registered to take the NCLEX on September 19, 2003, and my son was due for delivery on September 25, 2003. Six days apart, therefore, I could not stop thinking about labor pains. I was praying to God not to get labor pains before the exam. I worked with a tight schedule. Honestly, I had no idea about the monstrous NCLEX exam, never read a book about that exam. The only thing I had going for me was the hunger for success. THE STRONG DESIRE TO SUCCEED! I was desperate to pass that exam before giving birth to my son.

I requested NCLEX preparation materials. I received the KAPLAN REVIEW books and decided to read like crazy. I did thousands and thousands of questions; I believed in myself. My advice for those planning to take the NCLEX, please practice thousands of review questions. Understand why you are right and why you are wrong. Understand the rationale behind each question and each answer. For more information about the NCLEX, you can check out Janet Rangi on YouTube.

Do not just read textbooks, do as many sample questions as possible because the chance of failing will be very high if you only read nursing textbooks. In fact, you might fail. It does not matter the kind of review company you chose. Choose one and flip pages cover to cover at least 3 times. Test yourself and ensure you score above 89% before sitting for the NCLEX. I love the American education system; at the end of the day, the system ensures you know your stuff. No tricks because the goal is to master the necessary knowledge and understand where to get resources if needed in any situation.

Enough of that, how did I prepare for this examination? My routine was to wake up, take a shower, eat, read, sleep, read, you get the point. The nurses from the Philippines would wonder how I was going to pass the exam while pregnant, but I never wavered. I was always confident about my abilities, regardless of my situation. My prayer was to get through the exam without labor pains. Finally, I sat for the five-hour examination on September 19, 2003. At the end of the exam, the examiner gave me a big hug because I was nine months pregnant.

According to the examiner, I never turned my head during the exam. I was totally focused on the computer screen for five hours. Two days later, my English teacher came to the cafeteria where I was having lunch. She looked excited, "where is Janet! Where is Janet"! I was at the lunch table with my Filipino nursing friends. "Janet you passed! You passed"! The Filipino nurses were in shock, in dismay about how this young woman from Africa had arrived in America and passed the NCLEX in less than one month. My friends it's called determination.

My labor pains arrived six days after passing the NCLEX. I had no health insurance; I had no choice but to call the ambulance. That's beside the point — a story for another day. I finally gave birth to my son on September 25, 2003. It was a nightmare raising a child alone. The rest was history. I was licensed in the State of Nevada as a Registered Nurse after passing the NCLEX. I never worked in Nevada, but I used my Nevada license to endorse for a registered nurse license in New Jersey.

Remember the employer who offered me the job while I was still in Kenya? This employer was Salem Community Hospital of Salem County in New Jersey. This employer gave me a life changing opportunity in the United States. In return, I worked for the hospital for 4 years, including lots of overtime because the nursing shortage was so critical. I made more money working extra hours.

Many people will be interested to know how I changed my status from F1 student visa to green card. The short answer is the hospital petitioned immigration papers on my behalf. With the help of my sponsor and an immigration attorney, they changed my status from F1 student visa to permanent resident commonly known as green card. During the change of status, I was not required to attend school. In fact, the attorney filed for a work permit as I waited for the green card. I used the work permit to obtain a social security number and a driver's license.

Meanwhile, I did not need the green card to work. All I needed was the work permit. In a nutshell, it took less than 6 months between passing the NCLEX and starting to work officially. This period could have been shorter, but unfortunately, I experienced some personal difficulties during the process.

My green card finally arrived about one- and one-half years after petitioning. I resided in the United States continuously for 5 years after the green card then I applied to become a United States Citizen. I became a Citizen in September 2010. As you can see, this was a lengthy process but that did not stop me from my dreams. I know some took an easier path to work as nurses in the United States. They took nursing exams before coming to the United States. In my opinion, that is a better and less painful process because immigration is a beast; it's not for the faint hearted therefore, it is important to reduce any source of unnecessary stress.

How foreign trained nurses can get licensed and work in the United States

So, let's get down to business; one can become a nurse if they have a desire for that. However, nursing is a calling, and despite the benefits it offers, it's not a profession people should join blindly. I always recommend for people to choose one board of nursing in the United States and review the general requirements needed from foreign trained nurses. This will ensure the nurse is on the right track as she prepares to immigrate to the United States. For a start, you must attend university or college for 3-4 years. Make sure you take comprehensive general nursing courses that will cover all subject areas. Specializations such as psychiatric nursing or midwifery will not be accepted. You will need a nursing diploma or nursing degree from accredited Universities and Colleges, CGFNS will determine if your school is accredited before approving your Visa Screen.

To get a green card, you must be a registered nurse in your country; you must have a nursing license from the board of nursing, also known as Nursing Council in some countries. Let me stress this; a license is MANDATORY, do not skip this step. After meeting the education and licensing requirements, there are two ways to go about getting a nursing license in the United States. The first method I call the **DO IT YOURSELF** method... First Go to CGFNS International website.

After CGFNS International completes your credential evaluation process, they will provide you with a visa screen, which you will present to the board of Nursing of your choice within the United States. For demonstration purposes, let's look at the Texas Board of Nursing. Texas will explain what they require from foreign trained nurses. Just follow directions until they permit you to test for the NCLEX. Once you pass the NCLEX, Texas will give you a license.

The **DO IT YOURSELF METHOD** comes with challenges. First, how will the foreign trained nurse arrive in the United States? Under which visa category? How will this foreign nurse identify hospitals that sponsor foreign nurses? Well, the nurse can try to get the F1 student visa like I did or attempt to get a visiting visa. Remember, this will not be guaranteed because the embassy can deny a visa. Moreover, this nurse will be required to attend school while on a student visa. Each visa category comes with serious implications. Again, finding a hospital that sponsors foreign nurses will present another huddle for those wanting to place matters in their own hands. So how can you evade these obstacles while trying to migrate to the United States as a nurse?

I personally prefer using method number two, which I call the **AGENCY METHOD**. In the earlier chapter, I promised to share the names of recruiting agencies. There are several international nurse recruitment agencies; you must do your research; for me, I came across two examples of interest.

I came across Avant Health Care professionals and Adevia Health. I don't know these nursing recruitment agencies personally, but in general terms, agencies already have connections with potential hospital employers and immigration attorneys. Each agency of your choice will guide you through the application process. Once you pass the NCLEX exam, they will help you to get the green card. If needed, all immediate family members will accompany the nurse coming to the United States. Immediate family members include your spouse and unmarried children under 21 years of age.

I hope you enjoyed and learned from my personal story. Through my story, I share the process of coming to America as a foreign trained nurse. After securing the nursing job, nurses are privileged to get a green card, and eventually, they can choose to petition for the American Citizenship. Green card holders can get American Citizenship if they reside in the United States continuously for 5 years. Within those five years, they can travel outside the United States but not for a period exceeding 6 months. Once they become citizens, they can travel if they wish.

Using Nursing as a pathway to Citizenship if already in the United States

For those already in the United States without a green card, it's important to learn more about nursing training. There are different levels of nursing. Be aware that you can only get a green card if you are a Registered Nurse. Nothing less in terms of education. First and foremost, we have Certified Nurse Assistant commonly known as CNA. This is a good option for starters. You can obtain training on the job. Some places will offer about 6 weeks of training. Generally, CNA's assist the registered nurse in the hospital or nursing homes. The pay is usually low, but jobs are readily available. I like when new Americans start with CNA because it gives them exposure into the nursing field before they decide if nursing is a good career path for them.

The second level is a Licensed Vocational Nurse or Licensed Practical Nurse commonly referred to as LVN or LPN. These nurses are trained at a higher level than the CNA. These ones must go to school for about 2 years. They work in hospitals, nursing homes, outpatient clinics, schools, prisons and much more. Their salaries are much higher compared to CNAs. However, many healthcare facilities encourage them to continue with education in order to become Registered Nurses. Some places will not hire LVNs or LPNs. Kindly note that you will not be sponsored by a hospital for a green card if you only have CNA or LVN, you need to be a Registered Nurse in order to apply for the green card.

Registered nurses also known as RN's must have attained 3-4 years of nursing training in college or university and acquired a degree or diploma in nursing. After graduation, they are expected to pass the NCLEX examination and then get licensed. They coordinate with the doctors and other medical practitioners. Their Salaries are very competitive. For people already in the United States and who do not possess a green card, this could be a good pathway for them to become permanent residents and eventually United States Citizens.

So, once you pass the NCLEX, you can be sponsored by the hospital to get a Green card. RNs mostly work 12hour shifts 3 days or 3 nights per week, making nursing a very attractive career for raising a young family. Nurses can work overtime and make more money because of the critical shortage of manpower in this profession. Many nurses suffer from fatigue and burn out after working several years. Some elect to work as traveling nurses to make more money.

Nurse Practitioners, also known as NPs, are nurses trained at a masters or doctorate level in nursing. They are trained to do the same job as medical doctors but NOT surgeons. Nurse Practitioners generally make six figure salaries. Honestly, most employers prefer to use them because they offer the same services as doctors, but they are very cost effective. Meaning they offer medical services for less money compared to medical doctors. Although uncommon, these groups of nurses can maybe find an employer to petition for them the H1B visa.

So, let no one discourage you. Find a community college near you and start somewhere. An important note for those with bachelor's degrees in subjects other than nursing. They can go through Accelerated Nursing programs to obtain a bachelor of Science in Nursing, also known as BSN. For instance, it does not matter if you have a first degree in linguistics, history, international studies, engineering or law from any accredited University around the world, you can still become a nurse by building on previous knowledge.

Accelerated programs can propel you to a faster pathway in the nursing profession. Discuss with a school counselor about the accelerated nursing process. If you have good grades, there is a chance that the Universities will accept credits from your previous academic transcripts. For instance, let's look at the Wilson School of nursing Wichita Falls Texas that has accelerated Nursing programs.

I hope this Chapter has been an eye opener and I can't wait to hear about your future success with these programs. Nursing is just one of my career choices. I said it's one of the main pathways to get a green card and eventually United States Citizenship. I hope through sharing my story that some of my readers will benefit and use this as a pathway to shape their personal and professional careers. For those who follow my work, the goal here is to leave you better than I found you, it's all about having a strong desire to succeed.

JANET RANGI

MAKING THE RIGHT CHOICE

Understanding The Different Kinds Of Visas Available In The United States

B1/B2 VISA VISITING/TOURIST/BUSINESS VISA

One of the most common questions I receive is how long can I stay in the United States on a B visa? From what I gathered the immigration officer at the port of entry will decide how long you can stay and travel anywhere in the United States. You may return to the United States if the visa is valid and with no broken immigration laws.

It's important to mention that applying for a visiting visa takes a shorter period compared to other kinds of visas. This makes it very attractive for many applicants to apply thinking this is a gateway to live and work in America permanently. However, according to the laws in the United states, people cannot work using a visiting visa. You will not be issued a work permit or a social security number on a visiting visa. Healthcare is very expensive and therefore think twice when applying for visiting visa. Know your true intentions before embarking on the visiting visa request from the embassy. The truth is many people are in the United states working "under the table "because they have no legal means to live and work in the United States. Remember not to overstay your visa because this will jeopardize negatively any future applications with the immigration. They might deny you entry in the United States if you overstay your visa. If you want to stay longer, there are legal ways for you to do this, therefore, remember to request extensions or change of status in a timely manner.

Many people write to me requesting invitations to the United States but obviously that is not possible because I have thousands of followers. However, I am here to inform you about other ways you can come to the United States without depending on family, friends, and relatives. For example, conferences are a good way for you to obtain a B visa to the United States. Look at the variety of events and conferences that are being mentioned. The events and conferences cover a variety of professional fields all year through.

For example, 10times website has tones of events and conferences around the world but specifically, you will find events and conferences in the United States. Other common ways you can come on a B visa include wedding ceremonies and visiting popular attractions in the United States such as Disney world, Yellow Stone, the Grand Canyon among thousands of other fascinating places in the United States. Graduation season is also a wonderful opportunity for you to get invited if you have family and friends in the US; they can send you an invitation letter for you to come. They will write an invitation letter which you will take to the embassy together with other required documents. This letter should be short, succinct, simple and straightforward. Here is a sample of an invitation letter you can use for the embassy.

EMBASSY SAMPLE LETTER

Date (Type today's date)

Dear consular officers.

RE: REQUEST FOR A TEMPORARY VISA TO THE UNITED STATES

My name is Janet, and I live in Texas. I am inviting my cousin to come to my graduation. I will take care of her expenses during her stay in the United States. My cousin has a copy of my passport and driver's license. She also has a copy of my graduation letter from the University Registrar's office.

Kindly assist her accordingly. Thank you for what you do every day.

Sincerely Janet Rangi

Can I change The B visa to F1 Student visa while in the United States?

So now let's talk about when you already got your B visa, and you have arrived in the US. Can you change your status from B visa to other kinds of visas? The answer is yes, in fact, I have my followers who have listened to my advice and have gotten approved. Remember visa approvals are not guaranteed, the immigration officer can approve or deny your request to extend your visa or change your status from visiting to student.

But then again you must be smart on how you go about this you just can't be in the country for one day on B visa and then on the second day, you are at the USCIS website trying to change your status. As one is about to change their current B visa to F1 visa for students, you must first identify schools that know all about international students and visit the USCIS website on how to change and extend your B visa Status.

STUDENT F1 VISAS

I'm going to write about an important topic because I know this is reality. When you come to the United States on any kind of visa and specifically as a student, you need to plan. This is because student visas are expensive. Foreign students are required to stay in school full time to maintain their visa status. Staying in school involves paying tuition and maintaining good grades. You must plan because we don't want anyone to get deported. If you are very close to your family member and think you can't live without your family member; immigration is not for you. It's very hard, it needs a lot of resilience, and you are going to be apart from your family probably for a very long time. If you cannot handle separation from family and friends don't even, try it. Some of you probably for many years, you used to wonder that what happened to my uncle? He went to America for 20 years, and he has never come back? The thing is sometimes if your uncle did not plan accordingly, then he is unable to depart the United States because he does not possess the necessary visa to bring him back to America. Your uncle overstayed his visa and the best option for him is to stay inside the United States and work illegally.

I'm preparing you for student visas because many of you will probably not win the green card. I wish you well and hope that most of my followers will win the green card, but if we don't, we are going to be ready. People think that getting a visa after admission to community college is difficult. You must try your luck so long as community colleges continue to issue 1-20 to international students. Everyone is different and if you allow me to choose for you, aside from the green card, I will always choose a student visa because the visa opens many other ways to stay in the United States permanently. Like I said, F1 is common and usually expensive. You must prove that you have enough finances to cover your studies in the United States. This is done by showing back statements that reflect what the school is asking. However, you do NOT have to pay the full year once you arrive in the United States. I say this because followers have concerns about having the money to cover tuition for the full year. You will be required to pay fees according to credit hours. For example, if one credit hour will cost 250 dollars then multiply the 250 dollars with 12 credit hours each semester. Other expenses will be for your food and accommodation which you may get from other sources like relatives and friends. Some schools have payment plans, scholarships and other resources for you to get roommates. Always visit the international and financial offices for more guidance if you are stuck. With F1 visa, you are looking for a degree such as Associates which is called a diploma in some countries. This you will apply from community colleges and bachelors, masters and a PHD are offered in Universities.

What are some of the benefits of F1 Student Visas in the United States?

I personally prefer F1 student Visa because there is enough to figure out your life. You can always continue enrolling in school and extending your visa. For instance, after your bachelor's degree and when your visa is about to expire, you can go back to school again and enroll for a master's program. Discuss with the international office and they will apply for an extension on your behalf with all this time at your disposal who knows. Things might happen; life changes, for example, you could find love, get a boyfriend or girlfriend and maybe eventually get married legitimately. The marriage can earn you a green card if your American spouse is willing to petition a green card on your behalf.

If you intend to stay in the United States with an F1 student visa and go to school, I would advise to get your first degree in nursing. This may provide a pathway to change your status from student to green card. However, if nursing is not your thing, then consider other professions. You will have to study at a doctorate level in order to increase your chances of attaining permanent residency. Many international students complete a doctorate degree and then use employers to apply for them HIB visa which is very competitive.

The good news with a student visa is you can work 20 hours per week on campus. After graduation, you are eligible to apply for a work permit under the Optional Practical Training (OPT). During OPT you may work anywhere in the United States for one year so long as you meet all the requirements for OPT. Remember to visit the USCIS website many months before graduation to learn about how to apply for the OPT.

Process of applying for Student Visas

This is the way it will work on any website you go to. I am a very practical person. I'm not taking anything for granted with my followers because some will ask simple questions like how to apply. You are going to look for a school in the United States. Community colleges are much cheaper than universities. You want to make sure you get an application in a community college or a university. Make sure when you go on the website, the first thing you look for is the admission. The second thing you look for is the international student, and under the international student, you are probably looking for graduates or undergraduates. Then you go to application. For example: you go to Houston community college, you go under admission, which is for everyone around the world. But you want to scroll down, go to international students. Is it undergraduate or postgraduate? And there will find an application form. When you reach the application, you follow directions. If you have a question, they always leave contacts. Do whatever it takes to make sure you make an application. Once you satisfy them, they may ask for a bank statement. Ask a bank statement from a family, a relative, or anyone willing to sponsor; show them you will be able to pay fees for maybe one year. After you finish the application, they will send you an I-20. This is the admission ticket, and this is what you will take to the embassy.

In fact, sometimes the embassy might not need an admission letter so long as you have an I-20. Before you have an I-20, you must be thinking to have a passport. Don't wait till you get the I-20 and you start running around to find a passport because this might delay your visa application. You should have a passport. You can use the passport to go across the border in a country closest to you. Don't be one of those people that shows up at the embassy with a clean passport like you have never gone anywhere when you have neighbors across.

You can even take a train. Go there to a neighbor country visit and come back. Have that foreign stamp in your passport. I'm not saying traveling is necessary, but it gives people the impression that you are well travelled. When I went to the embassy, my passport was so dirty and messy. I used to travel. I had been to Tanzania and Uganda, my closest neighbors. So, maybe I gave the embassy the impression that this person is well travelled and therefore not so desperate for America, she's been out there traveling places. When you have your passport and I-20 ready, what is the next thing? You are going to go to the embassy. The United States has embassies around the world.

How is H1B Visa related to Student F1 Visa?

Employers can petition for H1B visa, which is a lottery meaning it is not a guarantee that it will be approved. Most of the time, they give priority to those who have American doctorate degrees. After getting the HIB, the employer can file for you a green card. The H1B is good for 3 years and can be renewed for another 3 years, making a total of 6 years.

During these 6 years, hopefully, you will be lucky to get a green card. My visa jobs website is a useful resource for those looking to familiarize with those professions that will allow you to change your status from student F1 to HIB visa.

COMMON REQUIREMENTS BEFORE APPLYING FOR STUDENT F1 VISAS

Before applying for student visas, it's imperative to find out if the colleges or universities need English examinations. It's worth mentioning two common English examinations done by foreign students. First and foremost is the Test of English as a Foreign Language popularly known as TOEFL. I did this exam several times. I had to do TOEFL to get my Nursing License; I did TOEFL for my green card and before joining my Master's program at the University of California, Los Angeles (UCLA). Another common one is the IELTS. The International English Language Testing System. Some colleges will require SAT scores. Scholastic Aptitude Test or Scholastic Assessment Test if applying for a bachelor's degree. For those planning to apply for a master's degree, you might be required to complete the Graduate Record Examination, also known as GRE. You might be required to take other examinations depending on your major course of study. The schools will guide you on what is required.

THE EXCHANGE VISITOR J1 VISAS

What does exchange program mean? It means that you come, mostly on a J1 visa to learn and share cultural information with Americans and take it back home. Exchange programs provide J1 visas that will allow you to attend school, work for a short period of time and participate in cultural exchange activities. Examples of J1 visas include Au Pair, Camp counselor, college and university students, government visitors, interns, international visitors, physicians, professors, and research scholars. These J1 Visas require an employer or an institution to sponsor you before seeking the visa at the embassy.

Many exchange programs you will be allowed to work and get paid by sharing your culture with the people of America and the people of America will share with you. People that apply for J1 should be careful because in most cases, they must fulfill the home residency requirement by going back to their country for 2 years before they will be allowed back. When they give you a chance to visit America, you better keep your terms. When you sign those J1 papers, you know just what you are doing. People ask me if they can change their J1 visas to something else but from my research this is usually very difficult.

GREEN CARDS OR PERMANENT RESIDENCY IN THE UNITED STATES

B efore getting into the diversity visa lottery, let us understand that there several ways of getting green cards and not just the lottery. Nursing is a pathway to come to America with a green card, but it's also a calling, and not everyone can become a nurse. There are other professions with green card opportunities. For example, religious workers such as Pastors can get a job in the United States and petition for a green card. You can get a green card through marriage to an American citizen at which time your unmarried children under 21 may qualify for green cards. Some employers can file for you to get a green card if they are unable to find American Citizens to work for them. Asylum seeker; this is whereby individuals fear for their lives and are being targeted for persecution from their home country.

When you apply for asylum, they will give you a work permit. Some of my follower's fear persecution and therefore have applied for asylum after arriving in the United States. With asylum you must apply your first year upon arrival in the United States; otherwise you will be disqualified. You must petition as soon as you can, and after approval, you may apply for an immediate family including spouses and unmarried children under 21 years of age. From experience, followers have been waiting for green card approval years after applying for asylum. However, they have been issued work permits and therefore they are able to live and work in the United States as they wait for the green card. Refugees; this is done with Non- governmental organizations which may file green cards on behalf of refugees. Investing millions of dollars in American jobs may also earn you a green card. Lastly joining the Military can be the quickest way to get a green card, although the rules have been changing recently. This is not an exhaustive list but hopefully, you have gotten an idea about the various ways people become permanent residents and eventually United States Citizens.

THE DIVERSITY VISA LOTTERY

The diversity visa lottery is usually open during the fall season, that's from October to November. First and foremost, the visa is free so let no one tell you that you must pay for you to participate. Once it is announced, make sure your country is listed or allowed to apply. Once that is done, read through the instructions and follow the directions before starting to apply.

Apply only once let no one cheat you that entering your information twice will improve your chance of winning the visa what this will do is to eliminate you automatically. When filling your information, be truthful and honest also you should be consistence although. In case of a couple, both can apply but it should be once, and whomever wins takes the family. If you are a single parent, you also can apply.

If you are using an agent to apply for you, you are solely responsible for the information that will be filed in your application. Make sure before you send your application you double check everything is correct. A Green card doesn't have an age limit, regardless of your state i.e. pregnant or not green card does not discriminate so don't be discouraged.

A Green card comes with a lot of benefits like going to school for free, have health insurance, work and live anywhere in the US have a social security number, take loans.

Once the diversity visa lottery is advertised, I will post the link and make sure we all do what we are required to.

HOW TO MAKE DIFFICULT DECISIONS AFTER WINNING THE GREEN CARD.

If you win the green card lottery have a sit down with your spouse and discuss with them the benefits of the green card. Be sure to be nice to one another and try and see from their perspective especially if the husband is already financially stable. Men tend to worry so much about their financial stability and that of the family. Therefore, it is important to understand the benefits of the green cards. These benefits include;

- Free education for the children; Your kids will be treated like the other children in the US.

- Excellence health care; You will have good health insurance plus best hospitals to take care of you when you are sick.

- Good higher education with financial aid; The US has best universities and colleges in the world. Financial aid and loans are available for permanent residents.

- Jobs are available and it's easier for someone with the green card than someone who must line up for a work permit.

- You will be paid better than your current situation and have some extra disposable income to invest in other business ventures like buying properties.

- Lifestyle changes, simple things like water and electricity are available throughout.

- You can start your own business without having to know anyone. All you need is to register it with the correct office and start your business.

Always be honest and consistence and make certain that you fill in the information correctly. There are many examples I have come across after working with thousands of cases. I will give a few examples;

WHAT ARE THE COMMONLY ASKED QUESTIONS AND CONCERNS ABOUT DEALING WITH THE EMBASSY AFTER WINNING THE GREEN CARD?

I was having problems in my marriage and decided to include my boyfriend on the green card application instead of putting my husband's. Luckily, I won the green card.

Unfortunately, you will more than likely be denied the visa at the embassy because you are still legally married with a marriage certificate. The embassy will consider your application as fraud and will jeopardize your future applications. You should have included your husband and maybe divorced him later. You can also part ways after arriving in the United States. You could have gone to the US without him. Unfortunately, you lost a chance and left a negative record with the embassy

I filed for the green card as single because I did not have a marriage certificate with the mother of my three children. After winning, I married her and updated the DS 260 as married. I remained honest throughout the process and eventually, my green card was approved.

Congratulations, the embassy can see through cases like yours, and because of your honest and consistent information, the embassy awarded you the green card.

I was a single man who won the green card and updated my DS 260 after marrying my wife. Later she refused to cooperate. I have a son with her, but the embassy is not aware of my son.

The embassy will need to know about your son; otherwise, you will be denied the visa. Always include all your minor children on the applications because omitting them will be a serious mistake especially if they find out during the interview or in the future

Can a green card holder (permanent resident) wait to file citizenship marry and petition for his wife? Both are in America.

From my experience, United States Citizens and green card holders can petition green cards for their immediate family members, namely spouses, parents and children under 21 years old. This will be a personal decision whether to file while as a permanent resident or wait and file as a Citizen. It depends on your individual situation because Citizen benefits generally have a shorter waiting period compared to non-Citizens. The good thing of filing early you can maybe file for a work permit as you wait for your relatives' green card to be approved. More information can be obtained at USCIS or from immigration attorneys.

Is there a lottery for Canada and how do I apply for it?

Canada offers permanent residency to immigrants, but they do not call that Green card like the United States. Unfortunately, I am not an expert in Canadian immigration issues, and I have never lived there. However, I have heard people applying through the Canada express entry system where the Canadian government gives visas to immigrants based on education and experience in a variety of skills. Consider visiting or going to Canada for studies and learn more about permanent residency in Canada. I think you may be pleasantly surprised at the opportunities Canada is offering to immigrants from all over the world.

There was a site of paying some dollars to apply for you a green card is it legal or fake?

I don't know if they are fake because some websites do help people to apply and charge fees for filing a green card. Just be aware the US state department, and the Immigration warns people about scammers and fraud. You can file for the green card yourself and the state department offers the step by step information about how to file for the green cards. They even have a video for demonstration purposes. Keep in mind that applying for a green card is completely free of charge. However, some people are not computer savvy and do not understand how to take professional photos required for the application. Such people can recruit services from Cibber cafes or other experts to help with the application process. Understand that primary applicants are responsible for the information that will show up on the application form. It's, therefore, imperative to review the application before submitting. Always make sure the person assisting with the application enters all the information accurately. Make sure they include your personal email and save your confirmation number.

I've been longing to immigrate to the States for long. Please enlighten me on ways that can enable me to get a visa.

In my videos, I talk about immigrant and nonimmigrant visas. Immigrant visas will enable you to move to the United States permanently; they are called permanent residency visas or well known as green cards. People get green cards in many ways, through the well-known lottery announced October of each year. Some get green cards because they have extraordinary talents such as world known athletes, university professors and researchers. Some people have life-changing inventions or discoveries and can get green cards. Some people have millions of dollars and can start a business in the United States; therefore, they get green cards. Some get green cards through employment, such as nurses and physical therapists. Some get married to US citizens and permanent residents and get green cards through spouse or fiancée visas. United States citizens and permanent residents can petition for their immediate relatives to get green cards. Spouses, parents and unmarried children under 21 years old are considered immediate relatives. The waiting period after filing for an immediate family can be between 6 months to 2 years. Brothers and sisters can also get green cards, but the waiting period takes many years; sometimes it takes over 10 years for a citizen to bring his or her brother or sister. In these cases, sometimes the brothers and sisters decide to use other temporary methods of immigrating such as student visas. Other relatives such as Cousins, uncles' grandparents cannot benefit from family sponsorship because they are not considered family member regarding immigration. Some people venture into adoptions to petition for extended family members. Some get green cards through asylum and refugee status. Sometimes working for international organizations in the United States will enable you to get green cards.

Nonimmigrant visas are temporary visas and require you to return home after visiting the United States. These include Visiting for business or pleasure under B1B2 visa. Exchange programs provide J1 visas that will allow you to attend school, work for a short period of time, and participate in cultural exchange activities. Examples of J1 visas include Au Pair, Camp counselor, college and university students, government visitors, interns, international visitors, physicians, professors and research scholars. These J1 Visas require an employer or an institution to sponsor you before seeking the visa at the embassy. Finally, my favorite visas are student visas, which can be time consuming and expensive to apply. However, the dividends are worth your time and effort. Be aware that people can change from temporary visas to permanent visas after staying in the United States. Changing from temporary to permanent visas takes a process, and nothing is guaranteed. Many immigrants from all over the world became United States Citizens through these kinds of visas. These are just but a few ways how people immigrate to the united states. More information can be obtained at USICIS website

My wife won the green card and we did all the test, but my wife lied about our son. She is not the biological mother. The DNA proved that am the father of my son. Now we have been told that we can't come to America because of that one mistake my wife did. She loved my son, and she did not want to live him back home.

This is a very good question because so many people misunderstand the embassy and the American systems. These are humans and they understand situations, but at the same time, they try to do the right things and follow the law. Take heart because your wife loves your son as her own. Unfortunately, when they catch lies about children, it is very hard to overcome such mistakes. I am so sorry that you lost a good chance to meet your American dreams. You can apply again next time and acknowledge your mistakes, and hopefully, they will give you a second chance. Your son had a chance to come through other means because you as a green card holder could have eventually petitioned for him a green card so long as he remained unmarried and under 21 years. I understand the pressure of wanting to come to America with everyone but understand how things are done in the United States. Shortcuts can work sometimes but it is a matter of time before they catch up with you. Whenever in doubt, always consult with immigration lawyers and do not be afraid to write or call the embassy for questions. Remember you cannot be penalized for asking questions.

I have a son and his girlfriend won the green card but now the problem the girlfriend didn't include his details when applying for a green card. Do you think It's ok for them to do a civil wedding and get a marriage certificate and fill in the green card forms and attach the marriage certificate?

I think it is understandable by the embassy that people can get married after applying for the green card. They can update their new marriage in the DS 260 so long as the marriage is legitimate. Get a marriage certificate and keep it simple, straightforward congratulations. People get in trouble when they stop playing by the rules, but in this case, it sounds like your son has a right to marry his girlfriend and make the necessary changes needed by the embassy.

I am interested in applying for the next American green card lottery. I'm kindly requesting for the directions from you.

No problem follows Janet Rangi Facebook page I will post the link in October and November of each year when it opens. The reasons I post the correct links is to help people find the correct lottery website and avoid thousands of scammers on the internet. The link will come with all the directions you need to make your application.

I have been applying for a green card since 2014 thank God this year I have been selected but am still stranded on where to start the process. I would really appreciate help on how to go about it.

Congratulations my friend. Follow the message you received on the winning page they have instructions on how to complete the DS 260 forms. They will also guide you regarding the documents you will need and about the medical examination. You need to start looking for a passport and a sponsor who lives in the United States to house you when you land in America. If possible, find a sponsor that earns decent money. The United States has poverty guidelines; therefore, the sponsor will have to demonstrate that they will afford to support you financially. Be accurate and honest, and your chances of succeeding with the green card visa will not be an issue.

Hi Janet, I am married, and my husband is in the USA, been planning on how I can visit him before my citizenship is approved which may take even a year or so to go through. How can you help?

Congratulations, your green card is on the way, not your Citizenship. You must be a permanent resident for at least 3-5 years, depending on how you got a green card for them to issue citizenship. I understand your frustration waiting too long to see your husband. From experience, they deny visiting visas to applicants like you because they know you are taking a shortcut by asking for a visiting visa instead of waiting for the green card. You must demonstrate strong family ties back home for the embassy to issue a temporary visiting visa. In your case, you will demonstrate strong family ties in the United States; therefore, it's unlikely that you will return home. I hope this makes sense, but you might be lucky if you try a visiting visa, you have nothing to lose good luck.

My parents are US citizens they filed for an Immigrant Visa for me and went for the interview in but unfortunately for me, I was denied. The consular said I did misrepresentation of facts, so they advised me to let my parents look for an Attorney, so we applied for a waiver of inadmissibility which my parents did. God has been so good my waiver has been approved by USCIS. Please, I would like to know what is the next process which I am kind of Confused. Any advice for me after my waiver of Inadmissibility has been approved.

Congratulations I am glad you were finally approved if you meet obstacles an immigration attorney will be able to help as advised by the Consular.

I lost the number how else can I check if I was selected?

Go to the State Department website link for checking if you won the green card. On the side, click FORGOT CONFIRMATION. You will be prompted to respond to some of your personal information. Hopefully, you will retrieve your confirmation number.

I have not been selected for the DV lottery can I still check my entry status every month?

Sorry, but if you have the correct confirmation, it's unlikely that you will win again. Good luck tries again next time, never give up.

On our applications both mine and my husband, we indicated we married. My worry is we don't have a marriage certificate, but we've been together for like 24yrs with three children aged 20,15 and 12 years Will this disqualify my application when it comes to interviews if we among the chosen for the green card?

From your question I don't see if you will have a problem although you might want to legalize your marriage formally by getting a marriage certificate. That will make future applications easier for you. You have lived together for many years, and you have kids together. Provide your honest, straight forward story they embassy can see through such things. Common law marriage or traditional marriages are part of our society, consider legalizing your marriage going forward no need to panic

Please share information on what happens after one win. Most people think when they win a green card, the US Gov't will give a house, a car, a job and money to use. There is this story that a man had won a green card and when he landed at the airport, he was asking the immigration officer to give him a car, a house and the job they promised. Clearly this was a misunderstanding that the green card gives all the luxuries in life. Please talk to us about it and please educate people on this matter because many have a misconception about winning the Lottery.

Thank you for sharing, and I have made videos about green cards. Green card winners are required to find their own sponsors in the United States. They will have to demonstrate to the embassy that they have housing and someone willing to support them in the United States, the embassy will guide winners about what is required from their sponsors. The Us government does provide jobs or financial support to green card lottery winners.

I just found out I won the DV Lottery. I applied as single but set to marry soon. Can I marry and get to travel with him?

Yes, you can marry so long as your marriage is legitimate. Marriage is a human right, and I am sure the embassy knows that. Remember to update your DS 260 from single to married and obtain your legal marriage certificate.

Hello Janet, thank you so much for the information you share with us. Pardon me if I ask a question you've answered before. I'm married, and we have one child. Can we apply for a green card as a family or it must be either me or my husband?

Thank you for following and asking questions; You apply separate and include her as your wife and child, she applies separate and includes you as husband and child. You cannot apply twice, meaning the primary applicant cannot enter the same application more than once because that will lead to automatic disqualification.

Hello Janet. Hope this message finds you well. I have been lucky to be selected during the Green Card 2020. Now I have a question. Last year I had applied for a B1/B2 visa but unluckily the Embassy didn't grant it unto me. Can the B1/B2 affect the Green Card issuance during the interview?

Congratulations for winning. Relax and enjoy your winning because the B1/B2 application will not affect your chances of getting the green card visa in my opinion. Most people are denied green card visas based on issues such as previous visa violations, fraud and general dishonesty.

What if I got a green card and I'm dropout at high school, will I go to America?

The green card regulations require you to have a high school certificate in order to qualify for a green card lottery. If your spouse has high school education, you can still come to America based on your spouse credentials. In other words, marriage to a qualified principle applicant can be a gateway for high school dropouts to get a visa.

My wife has been selected for further processing in the DV program, but we are shocked to learn that registered nurse is categorized as JOB ZONE 3 yet they need one's occupation to be JOB ZONE 4. We are so stressed does this mean we are disqualified. My wife has a diploma in nursing.

From previous applications, your wife qualifies for a green card because she has more than a high school education. I have seen those categories too and I think it's better to wait and see how the embassy will issue visas for the green card lottery winners in the future.

If I win a green card and I want to come to America despite her not being part of the lottery application, can I include her?

If you are married or plan to marry be honest with the embassy, also update your DS 260 application to reflect marriage. There is nothing wrong with marrying, it is a universal right, and the embassy is aware of that so long as the marriage is legitimate.

I won, and my question is about the green card form. There a question asking for passport details. I fear renewing to the e-passport because I will not have any proof of the old one.

Congratulations for winning the embassy and the passport office will guide you no need to be scared.

JANET RANGI

INTERVIEWS AT THE AMERICAN EMBASSY

T here is no way for one to come to America without going through the embassy and getting the visa approved. I have invested time and energy online searching for information regarding the embassy and how the embassy officials make decisions. In my videos, I have often referred the embassy as the "BIG ELEPHANT IN THE ROOM ". The embassy decides people's fate when it comes to stepping on American soil. Because the Embassy decision to approve or deny a visa is so crucial, it's very important to understand how things work in the United States and specifically how these officials make their decisions. During my online search I came across some video clips of American embassy officials in India, Philippines and Nigeria. I listened very carefully to what they were saying and discovered some tips you can utilize when you visit the American embassy to request a visa.

Some of the questions the embassy officials were asked in interviews allowed me to have an inside deep understanding about how they make decisions. One of the officers said that their decisions to grant or deny a visa are based on United States immigration laws. The law assumes that applicants for temporary visas have the intention of coming to America with no plans of going back home. Therefore, the burden of proof lies upon the visa applicant. The visa applicants must prove that they have strong ties back home; those reasons should compel them to return home after completing their legal stay in America. There is no special magic here but everyone, in my opinion, has the responsibility to demonstrate to the interviewer what will make them go back home. Examples of compelling reasons include but not limited to having properties, having a good job or business, maybe marriage and having children. These are just but a few examples, the list cannot be exhaustive because take, for instance, a young unmarried student applying for a student visa. Such students get approved for a visa many times despite their age, joblessness and marital status. That is why I highly recommend filling the DS 160 forms completely and to the best of your knowledge. I believe those forms provide the most important clues as to whether to approve or deny the visa. The second most important aspect is the first impression when you present in person. In fact, from my research, I realized that the number of documents you have might not rely matter; they can still decide without the documents. The most important part is to complete the right forms, have a valid passport, pay the required fees and present for the interview. They focus on the reasons taking you to America and the intent you must return home after your stay in America. We know that we will be doomed if we cannot pass the embassy interview. Therefore, I emphasize on this topic today; no one can promise how the interview will go until you present yourself one on one at the embassy. There and then you will have an opportunity get an American visa. Nothing comes easy you are taking a risk, paying nonrefundable fees when applying for a visa at the embassy. Having said all this, I will share some tips based on having lived and worked in the United States for many years. I understand the American laws and culture and therefore following these tips may increase your chances of crossing the embassy successfully.

Before you step in the embassy, make sure you put your truth very straight. You don't have to change your truth along the way. You cannot say one thing today and you say another tomorrow. You must have your thing ready. You must know your marital status. For instance, some people are separated from their husband; they don't know whether they are married or not. And I tell them "If you don't have a divorce decree, you are still married so keep your story clean and straight to avoid the impression of lying.

After you apply, these are some of the main points you are looking for in the application:

Do a very good job with your DS 160 application. Describe well about your work duties. You will write clearly, and I think these days, you must type which is a good thing. If they ask you a question; be clear. Write "not applicable or nil." Don't leave blanks. Make it complete. Make the form very clear. When they can't understand what you have written on the form, it makes the person reviewing it angry, and we don't want them angry and irritable. You want to look at the photo requirements and have them ready. Have your transcripts from high school or college ready? If you did some English as a foreign language or Graduate Record exams, you want to have your results ready.

You need to have your bank statement to show your finances. You want to have your finances from your dad, mom, aunt or sponsor. If it is a sponsor, they must write a letter stating your relationship with them and how much they are willing to help you. The next step is to go to the embassy and wait. I have a letter from someone who got denied a student visa from the embassy and what was on the letter was the same thing I have always told you. The letter said you must have compelling reasons why you want to go to the United States and return home after graduation. Stuff like you must show family ties that will force you not to stay in the United States but return home after completing your mission. Remember when you apply for student visa; make sure you can speak good English unless your I-20 says you have a problem with English. In that case, they will expect you to have basic knowledge in English.

Be on time; after getting the date and time for the interview, be in time for your time so that you stay calm and relaxed, familiarize yourself with the place, time to put your things together.

Be organized; put all your document in an organized manner and have all the documentation that you think will help your process to go through smoothly and easily. Preferably put your things together the previous night before going to sleep.

Ambassador; be your own ambassador, when you go for the interview have a friendly face, smile, be organized, be audible example if you are going for a student visa show the interview why you deserve the visa to be approved by knowing all about the school you are going to but stick to the topic.

Be consistence; be aware of what you fill in your application and be honest, example you filed that you are going for a student visa then on the day of interview you talk about visiting your fiancé. With that, the interviewer will know you are not honest, and your visa will be denied.

Body language; body language is very important; it tells a lot about you. So, maintain eye contact, have a smile on your face, be firm. In this way, you are showing you are not serving, and you are confident in whatever you are saying. This might help with your application.

Do not try to influence the decision of the interviewer. Always stick to the topic being asked. Do not try to add things that you think might influence their decision to benefit you in most cases it might backfire on you. Do not try to explain unless you are asked to.

Honesty; you should be honest and consistency in the information you give out. If the interviewer sense that you are laying to him/her, your application will be automatically be dinned, remember any information you give out is documented on the computer.

Confidence; show confidence during your interview smile, relax if you are applying for student visa show them that you are a good student speak in a voice that they can here pay attention when you are being talked to, so they won't have to repeat the question repeatedly.

Maintain eye contact; this is a way of showing honesty and confidence in yourself. Do not cross your arm when talking as this show that you are done talking about any matter/conversation. It's all about culture.

Point to remember is that you cannot appeal for non-immigrant visa if denied. When your visa is denied never use the word "WHY" to ask for an explanation for the denial instead approach it in this way, "thanks for your time, I know my visa has been denied but could you please tell me what I can do to improve my application next time." The official might consider explaining why but based on my online research, they might just hand you a denial slip. The denial paper simply means you did not present strong ties that will compel you to return home at the end of your stay in the United States. If your visa gets denied never give up book for another appointment and try again. However, it's important to determine some of the material changes with your finances or personal life. In the next interview, they will want to know what is different from the time you were denied the previous visa, what changed for them to have a reason to give you a visa after getting denied. Always keep in mind that it does not hurt to be friendly, smile, be audible and strike a conversation with the interviewer. At the end of the day, they are also human beings. Strive for success and remember excuses are a polite way of accepting failure.

There is no time frame for you to reapply if your visa was denied, but according to my research, it advised to wait for at least 90-180 days before you apply again. This is to have time for you to gather all the documents needed and who knows maybe your situation might have changed since you were denied a visa.

Regarding the bank statement, they understand about social network in the United States, they are very aware that you may get help from family members, relatives or even friends. At the end of the day, it's how you present yourself at the interview, this is a chance for the embassy to translate your application into a real person.

Some have asked if there is a chance to be returned home at the American port of entry. Understand that the visa is permission to get through the door and most of the time, the officers at the port of entry will respect the embassy decision to issue a visa. It is most likely you won't be returned home if you show consistency as to why and where you are traveling to. At the point of entry, the officer will ask you some questions not because they don't have your information, but they want to hear you state why you are coming to the US. Your story and reasons to travel better match the information you gave at the embassy back home. Of course, you cannot carry documents demonstrating permanent move if you intend to visit America temporarily.

In case of human error; they understand human error can happen and it can be fixed; however they will automatically deny your visa if they sense lies or dishonesty, example 3 years ago you identified yourself as Mary then you return with a new passport as Jane, this will be a serious breach which will lead to denial.

COMMON QUESTIONS AND CONCERNS ABOUT GETTING VISAS AT THE EMBASSY

Is there a time frame when applying for a visa?

There is no time frame for you to reapply if your visa was denied, but according to my research, it is advised to wait for at least 90-120 days before you apply again. The concern will be what has changed since you were last denied a visa? Hopefully you can make your case stronger during this period. This is to give you time to gather all the documentation needed and who knows maybe your situation might have changed.

In our opinion what do they look for in bank statements that are not from the applicant?

Regarding bank statements, they understand about social networks because you may need help from your family members, relatives or even friends but at the end of the day how you present yourself and your case matters.

Is there is a chance to be returned home at the point of entrance to America?

According to my findings the visa is like permission to go ahead and knock on the American door. Most likely you will not be returned home if you show consistency in your reasons for travel, you have no criminal record and you have not involved yourself in fraud. At the point of entry, the officer there will ask you some questions not because they don't have your information, but they want to hear you state why you are coming to America therefore presenting consistent information is very important. The Port of entry officer will more than likely respect the decisions to grant you a visa at the embassy.

What if I have a mistake on my passport like names and dates of birth?

In case of human error, they understand human error can happen and it can be fixed but, in any case, if they determine lying on your part your visa may automatically be denied. For example, 3years early you identified yourself as Mary then you come back or represent your document with a different name then that's a denial. But if the passport office made alphabetical mistakes or mixed your dates of birth, they might give time to fix the mistake and then return to the embassy for a visa.

I started watching your videos after I had been denied a visa and since then I am still watching hoping to try again if another invitation comes. I want to weigh my options because my spirit keeps telling me to try again.

Thank you for watching my videos. You can apply for a visa as many times as you wish, but I think you will have to wait at least 3-6 months. This is because there must be a material difference in your lifestyle since the previous denial. What has changed financially or socially since the embassy denied you a visa? For instance, did you travel outside the country, did you get a new job, or maybe did you recently get married or have children? The reason for your visit must be compelling too. For example, an invitation to visit your brother could be less compelling compared to a conference that will give value to your country and the United States. The truth is your brother can always visit home if he has a legal visa in the United States. Another good reason for visiting is tourism, for instance, there is only one Niagara Falls and if your reason is to visit Niagara Falls, then this could be a better reason for travelling to the United States or Canada. Give yourself a chance by having more compelling ties to demonstrate your intention of returning home after your trip to the United States. From my experience and research, I realized the embassy looks at the totality of your application and who you are as an individual.

Carrying a load of documents such as title deeds does not make your case necessarily stronger. The most important documents are those that are required by the embassy. These include your DS 160 application, current passport, embassy fee payments, passport size photographs, and the document showing the reason for your travel. The rest of the documents such as tittle deeds you may carry just in case, they ask for them. I would recommend you complete your DS 160 application for the embassy interview honestly and very well detailed because this will be the first impression the embassy will have about you. Secondly, the DS 160 has questions designed by the United States, therefore, consider answering these questions in good details, use good grammar, and avoid spelling mistakes. They could ask questions from the DS 160 during the interview. Nothing is guaranteed my friend but keep try and never give up.

What are the frequently asked questions at the embassy because I am planning to go there, and I am really encouraged by your videos.

The DS 160 application should be a guidance as to what the embassy wants to know about you. It is more than likely that they will ask questions directly from the DS160 application for the interview. Generally, know the reasons for your travel, why the United States, where do you plan to stay, how will you fund your trip and be aware of all your family ties in the United States. If you have relatives and friends in the United States, how long have they been in the United States? What do they do for a living? Where do they stay, what is their visa status and when did you last see or speak with them? The embassy does not spend a lot of time asking questions during the interview because of the long lines; therefore, consider submitting a strong DS 160 application. The DS 160 application will be scrutinized before your interview, and this will become part of your embassy records for future reference. Remember consistency with your information will build trust between you and the embassy.

Can someone who was denied a visa after giving false information, apply again with genuine information?

You can apply again because we are human, and we make misstates. The embassy is operated by humans too, and you might be surprised that they will consider listening to your case. Apologize and say you learned your lessons, acknowledge your shortcomings and hope they will give you a second chance. You have nothing to lose by trying again.

Someone I call my Godmother in the US wants to invite me to visit her and I want to know the documents I will need to apply for the visa. She's ready to take care of everything my accommodation and flight, but I'm scared I might not get the visa. What should I do?

Apply for the B1B2 visa interview by filling the DS 160 truthfully and well detailed. Pay the requires fees then have your passport and passport size pictures as requested by the embassy on their website. The rest of the stuff like bank statements and invitation letters might be requested by the consular but do not necessarily make your case stronger.

Is it possible for somebody who is not a relative to invite me in America?

Yes, anyone can invite you to the United States so long as you have a relationship of some kind. The embassy will want to know the reasons for your travel. A letter of invitation may be required, but the embassy looks at your applications in totality.

Hello Janet, was hoping to have won the green card but now that I didn't, I will still go ahead and try to get there through other means...my question is can I access the DS 160 prior to going to the embassy for study? Just to make sure I fill up the correct information.

Sorry about the green card you can always try next time. Sorry about not winning the lottery. That's is why I advise people not to put eggs in one basket always have plan a, b and c which you seem to have. You can probably go fill the DS 160 to familiarize with the questions but do not submit it to the embassy.

My wife is currently in the USA and she filed for me a year ago, but we have not yet heard from the USCIS. The big deal is that she is currently pregnant; we kindly want your counsel on how to expedite the process for me to join her.

Congratulations on your pregnancy. Immigration issues are sometimes difficult, and we wish things could work in our favor. Most of the time they don't work in our favor, especially when it comes to USCIS processing times. I am not sure what kind of visa your wife applied for you. There is a system in place to check the visa processing times and you will know exactly how long to wait. Your wife can call the USCIS to find out if they have expedited services for your kind of visa application. Visa processing times can be found on the USCIS website. Keep in mind that the receipt notice was sent to your wife after she petitioned for you. The receipt has key information you will use to determine the processing times. Have that form ready before calling USCIS. This is the USCIS number to call 1 (800) 375-5283.

Good EVENING please I have a question I was approved after interview for nonimmigrant visa, but my status is currently under administrative processing what does that mean?

They need more information before making a final decision about approving your visa. Most of the time they will clear you, keep me updated, call or email them politely to find out if you don't hear from them.

Ok, it has been 50 days now since its administrative processing and I wasn't given any slip with more information needed or documents needed just administrative processing. Also, after my interview, I realize I made a mistake in other names I answered no, but my last refusal of US visa was with my former name I don't know if that is the cause of all this. Also, I was able to answer the question if I have been refused before I answer YES, so they can realize I never intended to hide my former name. I have no criminal or bad immigration records, no past convictions as well. Can these other names questions be the cause, is its material misrepresentation?

Okay I see call them or email them and state your name and passport number. State this in your email;

You placed me on administrative process, and I haven't heard from you ever since. Kindly let me know if there is anything, I can do to get the visa thank you. Make sure you update your reason for coming for example if it's visiting visa and the reason for the visit is over then it's tricky you might need another reason for visiting.

I am going for an f1 student visa to the united states embassy and my interview is around the corner.

All the best I hope you get the Visa kindly watch my embassy videos but overall understand everything you wrote on your DS 160 application. They might ask questions directly from that. Have all your documents., filing fees, passport, photographs and bank statements. They might not ask for all these things from experience they are busy dealing with long lines at the embassy, therefore, do a good job on your DS 160 application since that will give them a first impression about you.

We all know the embassy consular are very strict with us and I want to know how to go about it because am a first timer going to further my education. May I also pass greetings from my parent to you. We all take time watching YouTube uploaded video we all love you God bless your hand work.

Thank you so much and pass my greeting to your parents and thank you for watching. With education, you apply for F1 student visa. You need to identify a school that offers your kind of course or degree or something you like. Then visit their website and start an application for international students. They will guide about all you need to submit. After you submit your application and documents, they will decide for admission. If you are admitted, they will send you an I-20 which you will need to submit to the embassy during your interview. The embassy will guide what they need from F1 student applicants. You will need to pay SEVIs fee if they issue an F1 student visa. Good luck.

I went to the US embassy and my visa was approved. Days later, they called me back for another interview. They found out that my spouse was already in the US and was not even a citizen. I had said I was going for a conference. Someone told me to apply again. Should I change what I had written on my other DS 160

Wow, that was close because they issued the visa. Obviously, it seems that you had a strong case that is why they initially had issued the visa. Looks like they realized your strong ties were in the United States and not home. The embassy looks at making sure applicants have compelling ties that will make them return at home. You can apply as many times as you want, but I think they will want to know what has changed since the previous applications. In my opinion, student visas provide more value to the applicant than visiting visas. A conference provides more value to more people than visiting a family member who can come home to visit. Don't change stories; you will make your situation worse; it could lead to future denials. The embassy, like any other organization will obviously save information for future reference.

Today I've gone through almost all the videos posted here. I had many questions, but they have been answered by watching the videos. I can't see the file section to read more I have a deep desire to come to States. Motivation could be coz my job has ended, and I need to do something. Some questions that have been answered include: - Applying for a student visa at my age. I'm 46 years. I've seen you mention that they allow. Finances. I've raised a considerable amount of money Career. I want to change to be a nurse. Kindly advise

Very good, Green card so long you follow directions clearly it does not matter where The problem of someone applies for you make sure application is accurate and actually submitted only once, Age not issue, Not issue with age still young, Keep saving, Career does not matter come here first with best visa that's the most difficult.

I am 35years. Can I still qualify for visit visa? *Yes, you can qualify at any age 35 is very young, my friend.*

We have a family friend who got a tourist visa early last year and travelled to America. He decided he was not coming back, and he overstayed his visa.

It's hard to advise once someone overstays their visa, they might have a lawyer who is helping with the situation that is beyond my abilities

HOW TO GET FREE COLLEGE EDUCATION IN AMERICA

I am so surprised how much people talk about expensive college education and about the ballooning student loan debt, yet no one speaks about the real solutions to avoiding student debt. I say this because people do not have to borrow student loans if they plan and learn about some very important financial decisions that could reduce or eliminate student loan debt. It is possible to pay for college without borrowing any money. Here are a few strategies.

First and fore most it's important to establish your residency for a state because most colleges will charge less tuition if the students are residents of the state. Right here, some students end up paying expensive out of state tuition because they did not plan.

Second look for jobs benefits. Some jobs have tuition reimbursement whereby the employer will pay for your college if you promise to work for them for a certain number of years. To be honest, my employer is paying for full tuition for my post-graduate studies and in return, I will work at my job for three years. These are real-life examples; you are learning from someone who has lived the experience.

Third, be prepared to work in smaller towns and cities that are desperate to find workers because such places have limited talent, they are more likely to offer educational funding such as tuition reimbursement or loan repayment programs. For example, visit the National Health Service Corps to learn more about grants scholarships and loan repayment programs. My employer paid in full for my Master's program as a Family/Psychiatric Nurse Practitioner because I chose to work in a city that is difficult to recruit people with my kind of education.

Fourth it's important to know that community colleges are cheaper than universities and they tend to provide practical and hands on training. Because of the short nature of the courses provided by community colleges, they tend to receive financial assistance from the government and private companies looking to hire quick yet more practical talent.

Fifth, remember to always ask the financial office about what kinds of financial assistance is available, including scholarships, grants and loans. I honestly believe in "ask *and it shall be given, knock and the door will be opened for you* ". This happened to me I asked for help, and my University gave me scholarships for my university education, I have always wondered if I had not asked what would have happened. Most of my Master's tuition was covered by the University, the rest of the loan paid for my living expenses in the expensive Los Angeles. Again, you are learning from someone who has lived the experience.

Sixth, choose your courses wisely. This is tricky because some people will be passionate in more marketable courses than others. If you are one of those people who has no interest in a subject area, I will highly recommend venturing into STEM courses, - meaning Science, technology, engineering and Math. These tend to have more financial incentives. For those who choose to study Human sciences such and Nursing, medicine, dentistry, Pharmacy they are more than likely to receive tuition reimbursement and loan repayment programs. Personally, my employer offered loan repayment in full, remember the school gave me tuition assistance but the remaining loans were paid by employer just because I work as a Nurse practitioner in underserved populations. Let us look at another example of loan repayment programs for medical professionals. The National

Health Service Corps (NHSC) Kindly visit their website to learn more about loan repayment programs. Remember to check each state for loan repayment programs because *"information is power".*

Seventh look into student work programs on and off campus. Foreign F1 students can work 20 hours per week on campus. Master students can apply for CPT and work full time. Those with a work permit or those who are United States Citizens obviously can work as they go to school to reduce or eliminate student loans.

Eight take advantage of graduate assistantships for on campus employment. Students with previous academic experience can assist professors with academic work and get tuition payments in return.

Ninth if you have a passion of becoming a soldier joining the military could be a solution to paying for college. Although non-citizens or those without a green card may no longer be able to join the military, it's a good idea to stay informed because the laws may change, or your immigration status may change.

Tenth, we are going to come the right way. We are going to come smart. As a matter of fact, people have been coming smart already. We want to do things the right way. You want to look for the scholarships. I have always said it's much easier to find scholarships after admission to a university or college; I am highly against people asking for scholarships without trying to apply to schools. Talking of scholarships, I like this website called international scholarships

Finally, if you are a minority student, you may be eligible for more student aid programs available for minority students. Minority student includes but not limited to people of the black, Hispanic, Asian and Native American descent. Be sure to search online and speak with your school if they have any scholarships or financial aid for minority students. Examples of African American scholarships include The United Negro College Fund awards scholarships, grants, and/or fellowships to African American undergraduate, graduate, and post-doctorate students who show exemplary academic achievement. The Gates Millennium Scholarship Program awards scholarships to talented minority students with financial need. The Jackie Robinson Foundation is a national organization that provides opportunities for minority students to achieve their dream of higher education. For more information, visit their respective websites.

JANET RANGI

CREDENTIAL EVALUATION SERVICES

I write this regardless of your profession if you have a bachelor's degree in any field you may use credential evaluation services. First, be aware of foreign credential evaluation services which will conduct an evaluation of your bachelor's certificates and transcripts to verify your education standards. Employers, colleges, and Universities frequently use credential evaluation services to verify your education.

Before embarking on my post graduate studies at the University of Texas Rio Grande Valley, I was required to evaluate my foreign education. The school recommended World education Services also known as WES.

Another very useful credential evaluation service used by many international students in the United States is Educational Credential Evaluators or better known as ECE. I have friends and family in dentistry who used the ECE services. These foreign credential evaluation services will guide you through the process needed to evaluate your foreign credentials. The job will guide you if they need credentials from you. Know what they want and follow directions. If they need your credentials to be evaluated, that's what you will do. The colleges and Universities will also let you know which credential evaluation services they prefer, and that's what you will need to use. Most institutions will require documents to be sent directly from the credentialing evaluation service after the evaluation is completed.

COMMONLY ASKED QUESTIONS ABOUT JOBS AND CAREERS IN THE UNITED STATES

I dream to work and live in either Canada or USA. On employment visa, what are the necessities?

This is a very complicated question, first not much information about Canada from me but consider doing research about the Canada Express entry program. Regarding USA, it depends on the kind of Visa you will apply at the embassy. Some Visas may allow you to apply for a work permit while in the United States, but some visas do not allow people to work. That is why I have done many videos about different kinds of visas in the United States for you to choose a visa that suits you best. There is nothing as employment visa, you need to find a way to enter the United States legally and seek jobs from employers while in the United States.

I specialized as a food and beverage sales and management personnel and a barista by profession. I have worked in 5-star hotels. I would like to work in the US to grow my career. How can you advise me on means to get there?

Check out more information about J1 sponsors for cultural exchange programs. The hotels and hospitality industries in the United States sometimes are short staffed and therefore take advantage of the temporary J1 excahnge program visas to bring foreign workers to the United States. Some hotel websites will guide you through the process by providing the contacts they use to bring foreign workers through J1 sponsorship. You could also apply for a community college admission on a student visa and come to study for a food and beverage diploma. You can also apply for a business conference in food and beverages and see where that takes you in the future. All these are ways for you to advance your career.

My daughter has finished campus but no job. Please kindly help how she can get a job in the US.

Congratulations your daughter has completed campus, and I am glad you are looking outside the box and coming to American is an option for jobless youth. There are many kinds of visas that your daughter can apply and once she comes here, she will follow other processes that might enable her to find a job. Personally, I recommend student visas because they will give your daughter time to go to school and work as she finds other ways of living and working in the United States permanently.

I was asking if you know any job opportunity in Canada. Since I heard the prime minister of Canada wants 1million immigrants.

The Canadian government gives permanent residency to immigrants from all over the world through a program called express entry which scans qualified candidates according to their education and language abilities in English or French. Those who meet these requirements are invited for further interviews and may obtain jobs in Canada. All this is public information and can be obtained online. However, you must be careful because so many scammers on the internet are taking advantage of these Canadian permanent residency opportunities.

I have a certificate in Nurse aid or CNA can that certificate help me to secure a job in the states or can you advise me on what to do to come there

You will have to train for Certified nurse assistant (CNA) program after you come to America. Good thing you already have the experience that should not be a problem. CAN program are usually short approximately six weeks and you can start working as a CAN

Is catering a good course? If you can advise me. *If catering is what you love to do that is okay and has nothing to do with you getting a visa. The most important thing is for you to get admission and present yourself at the embassy. It just depends on how you present your case because the embassy is the most difficult part for most applicants.*

OTHER COMMONLY ASKED QUESTIONS ABOUT THE UNITED STATES

I started watching your videos after I had been denied a visa and since then I am still watching hoping to try again if another invitation comes. I want to weigh my options because my spirit keeps telling me to try again.

Thank you for watching my videos. You can apply for a visa as many times as you wish, the question will be having there been any material difference since the previous denial. What has changed financially or socially. For instance, did you travel outside the country, did you get a new job, or maybe did you recently get married or have children. Give yourself a chance by having more compelling ties to demonstrate your intention of returning home after your trip in the United States

Hello Janet, need more information about this. Can a green card holder (permanent resident) waiting to file citizenship marry and petition for his wife? Both are in states

United States Citizens and green card holders can petition green cards for their immediate family members, namely spouses, parents and children under 21 years old.

Is there a lottery for Canada, and how do I apply for it?

Canada offers permanent residency to immigrants, but they do not call that Green card like the United States. Unfortunately, I am not an expert in Canadian immigration issues, and I have never lived there.

However, I have seen and heard people applying through the express entry system where the Canadian government gives visas to immigrants based on education and skills set

Hello, I hope you well what the most asked questions at the embassy planning to go on July am really encouraged by your videos

The DS 160 should be a guide as to what the embassy wants to know about you. It is more than likely that they will ask questions directly from the DS160 and DS 260. Generally, know the reasons for your travel, why the United States, where do you plan to stay, how will you fund your trip and be aware about all your family ties back home and in the United States.

I dream to work and live in either Canada or USA. On employment visa, what are the necessities.

This is a very complicated question, first not much information about Canada. Regarding USA, it depends what kind of Visa you will apply and get at the embassy. Some Visas may allow you to apply for a work permit while in the United States, but some visas do not allow people to work. That is why I have done hundreds of videos for people to learn more about different kinds of visas and apply those that suit them best.

There was a site of paying some dollars to apply for you a green card is it legal or fake?

I don't know if they are fake because some websites do help people to apply and charge fees for filing a green card. Just be aware the US state department and the Immigration wars people about fraud. You can file for the green card yourself, and the state department offers the step by step information about how to file for the green cards. They even have a video for demonstration purposes. Keep in mind that applying for a green card is completely free of charge. However, some people are not computer savvy and do not understand how to take professional photos required for the application. Such people can recruit services from Cibber cafes or other experts to help with the application process. Understand that primary applicants are responsible for the information that will show up on the application form. It's, therefore, imperative to review the application before submitting. Always make sure the person assisting with the application enters all the information accurately. Make sure they include your personal email and save the confirmation number.

And can someone who was denied a visa after giving in false information, apply again with genuine information?

Yes, you can apply again, we are all human and we make misstates. The embassy I think, understands that. You can apologize and say you learned your lessons acknowledge your shortcomings and hope they will give you a second chance. You have nothing to lose by trying again.

I've been longing to immigrate to the states for long. Please enlighten me on ways that can enable me to get a visa; I know some of them like the students Visa send me a variety of other ways because I've relatives in the states.

In my videos, I talk about immigrant and nonimmigrant visas. Permanent visas will enable you to move to the United States permanently; they are called permanent residency visas or well known as green cards. People get green cards through many ways, through employment, marriage to US citizens and permanent residence, through asylum, through refugee status. Sometimes working for international organizations for many years in the United States will enable you to get green. Nonimmigrant visas are temporary and require you do business in the United States and return home. These include Visiting for business or pleasure. Exchange programs that will allow you to work for a short period of time. Finally, my favorite visas are student visas, which are can be time-consuming and expensive to apply for, but the dividends are worth your time and effort. It is worth pointing out that people can change from temporary visas to permanent visas after staying in the Unite Sates for a while. This are just but a few ways how people immigrate to the united states.

My wife won the green card and we did all the test, but my wife lied about our son. She is not the biological mother. The DNA proved that am the father of my son. Now we have been told that we can't come to America because of that one mistake my wife did. She loved my son and she did not want to live him back home.

Take heart that your wife loves your son as her own. Unfortunately, when they catch lies about children, it is very hard to overcome such mistakes. I am so sorry that you lost a good chance to meet your American dreams. You can apply again next time and acknowledge your mistakes and hopefully, they will give you a second chance

In 2016 was in USA for J1 program and returned home and finished my education. In 2017 I retuned again to Chicago with 5yrs b1/b2 for few months contract. Later I returned home. my friends give me pressure that am sitting on five-year visa in my house and others are looking for such. Now you can't know how sometimes I feel guilty. But also, I do follow your teachings all the time and wonder when the time is coming for me to return to the USA.

Your case is strong because you have not violated the visa conditions. Nothing is guaranteed but your records are excellent. Your good history will give you an edge when applying for immigration benefits. Like everything else in life, we take risks. The question is then It is possible to change from B visas to student F visa. First, you need to approach the admission office of approved SEVIS colleges or universities and request admission. They will require your education credentials and a bank statement to show funding for your education. Once you meet all your requirements you and the school will file for the b visa extension and change of status from B visa to student F 1 visa. During the change od status, you will not be allowed to go to school or work. Once the changes are approved, you can start school. Some school will advise you to go back home and get a student visa stamped on your passport. Sometimes USCIS will approve your request and there will be no need to go back home. In this case, you can start school after you are approved.

Hi Janet, I know you are a busy person and I pray you could answer me this. I applied for community college, and they want a bank statement with at least $18200. Does it have to be from home, or I can ask a friend who is in the US to help me with hers? Or can I ask someone to just deposit that cash then withdraw just to send it to the college

The bank statements do not have to be from your home country. You can use a bank statement from anywhere so long as someone is willing to be your sponsor. The sponsor may be required to sign the financial forms. Direct deposits may be a red flag. Bank statements should have normal transactions as not to raise any eyebrows. At the end of the day the school needs a bank statement to reflect the amount they need.

Please how can you be of assistance to me? I need a conference to attend in Houston TX on a partnership with universities in the US, particularly in Texas.

I have posted links but quite honestly your question is specific and does not require someone who has lived the experience, you can easily find your answers on google. Thank you for asking.

Someone I call my Godmother in the US wants to invite me to visit her and I want to know the documents I will need to apply for the visa. She's ready to take care of everything my accommodation and flight, but I'm scared I might not get the visa. What should I do?

Nice to meet you they need you to apply for the interview by filling the DS 160 truthfully well detailed then pay fees then have your passport and pictures as requested. The rest of the stuff like bank statements and invitation letters they might not ask but carry good luck watch my conference videos Janet Rangi YouTube.

Hello, I have a visa interview in June for a visit visa, which documents should I bring along?

They need you detailed DS 160 your passport photographs and passport itself and payment the rest of the documents like invitations and bank statements they might not even ask but carry good luck I have had more success with business conference visas.

Hello Janet, this is my first time to hear you through Facebook video link, and I am humbled by your incisive discussion humble query is do you have any info on sponsors from that part of the world who are blessed and can sponsor needy student who have sat high school exams but due to poor background are unable to further their education?

Most of the time, you need to have admissions to look for sponsors. I hope you are learning and acting the best way is to start the process and let blessings meet you along the way.

Is it possible for somebody who is not a relative to invite me in America? *Yes, your relatives can invite you to the United States. You also can visit just because you want to sightsee or attend a conference.*

Hi Janet, I will be turning 40 this year and have dream to end up in Canada, Australia, New Zealand or States someday. I have no idea how to go about it. Do you have a link where I get the information to see if I qualify for anything? Thanks?

The link is my free videos learn about USA and act on your thoughts good luck.

My wife is currently in the USA and she filled for me a year ago, but we have not yet heard from the USCIS. She will be due for her citizenship in July 2019. The big deal is that she is currently pregnant; we kindly want your counsel on how to expedite the process for me to join her.

Congratulations on your pregnancy, sometimes we wish things could work in our favor. Most of the time they don't, especially when it comes to USCIS. I am not sure what kind of visa your wife applied for you. Having said that there is a system in place for you to check the visa processing times and you will know exactly how long to wait. Your wife can call the USCIS to find out if they have expedited services for your kind of visa application. Visa processing and your receipt notice that was sent to your wife after she petitioned for you has key information you will need to determine the processing time. Have that form ready before calling USCIS. This is the USCIS number to call 1 (800) 375-5283.

I am interested in applying for the next American green card lottery. I'm kindly requesting for the directions from you

No problem follow the page I will post the link in October and November of each year when it opens. The reasons I post the correct links is to help people find the correct website and avoid thousands of scammers on the internet.

I have been applying for a green card since 2014 thank God this year dv 2020 I have been selected but am still stranded on where to start the process.... I would really appreciate for help on how to go about it.

Congratulations my friend. Follow the message you received on the winning page they have instructions on how to complete the DS 260 forms. They will also guide regarding the documents you will need and about the medical examination. You need to start looking for a sponsor who lives in the United States to house you when you land in America. If possible, find a sponsor that earned decent money. The United States has poverty guidelines thereof the sponsor will have to demonstrate that they will afford to support you financially. Be accurate and honest, and your chances of succeeding with the visa will not be an issue.

Hi Janet, I am married, and my husband is in the USA, been planning on how I can visit him before my citizenship is approved which may take even a year or so to go through. How can you help?

Congratulations your green card is on the way not your Citizenship. You must be a permanent resident for at least 3-5 years depending on how you got a green card for them to issue citizenship. I understand your frustration waiting too long to see your husband. From experience, they deny visiting visas to applicants like you because they know you are taking a shortcut by asking for a visiting visa instead of waiting for the green card. You must demonstrate strong family ties back home for the embassy to issue a temporary visiting visa. In your case, you will demonstrate strong family ties in the United States, therefore, it's unlikely that you will return home. I hope this makes sense, but you might be lucky if you try a visiting visa, you have nothing to lose good luck.

Can the change of passport affect embassy interview?

From what the embassy posted on the website they are still using the old passports. If this changes, the American embassy is very good at communicating changes.

My parents are US citizens they filed for an Immigrant Visa for me and went for the interview in, but unfortunately for me I was denied. The consular said I did misrepresentation of facts, so they advised me to let my parents look for an Attorney, so we applied for a waiver of inadmissibility which my parents did. God has been so good my waiver has been approved by USCIS. Please, I would like to know what is the next process which I am kind of Confused. Any advice for me after my waiver of Inadmissibility has been approved. Thank You.

Congratulations I am glad you were finally approved, don't worry too much this time things will work well if you just keep a straight story, be honest. Thank you so much for following. If you meet obstacles, an immigration attorney will be able to help as advised by the Consular.

May you help me know more about your programs am really interested?

I hope you are watching and learning from my free videos on YouTube and Facebook. Thank you so much for following

Hello Janet, I am a fourth year at the University, and have I have wanted to move to Canada. I have been listening to your past videos concerning Green cards. I need to know whether I can join any university there and still get my completed credits done. I have five more credits to go so that I finish my undergraduate degree.

Since you are very close to graduating, maybe it's a good idea to wait and graduate before applying for student visas. But if you get a chance for F1 visa take it because some schools can transfer some of your credits if you scored well above a C in the subjects. Transfer credits will vary from school to school. As for the green card, it's a lottery therefore apply. You will graduate before the green card is processed.

Please I have a question I was approved after interview for a nonimmigrant visa, but my status is currently under administrative processing what does that mean?

They need more information before making a final decision about approving your visa. Most of the time they will clear you, call or email them politely to find out if you don't hear from them.

Ok it has been 50 days now since its administrative processing, and I wasn't given any slip of more information needed or documents needed just administrative processing. Also, after my interview, I realize I made a mistake in other names I answered no, but my last refusal of US visa was with my former name I don't know if that is the cause of all this. Also, I was able to answer the question if I have been refused before I answer YES, so they can realize I never intended to hide my former name. I have no criminal or bad immigration records, no past convictions as well. Can these other names questions be the cause? is its material misrepresentation?

Okay call them or email them and say" my name is so passport number. You placed me on administrative leave, and I haven't heard from you ever since. Kindly let me know if there is anything, I can do to get the visa thank you" Make sure you update your reason for coming for example if it's visiting visa and the reason for visit is over then it's tricky you might need another reason for visiting.

If I have a bachelor's degree in laboratory and would like to change to nursing so can I use my Bachelor's to apply for nursing degree course if I can't be given bachelor's in nursing what do you think I can be given?

You can always change to Nursing after you arrive in the United States. Visit the school counselor and they will guide you how to start the process

I have been denied visa three times, I'm single but I put in married in my form with a child because I thought that might give me a chance to have a visa. I still want to come to America so my question is if I want to apply for a green card should I still say I'm married with one kid when filling the green card form?

Since you said married with a child on the initial application sticking with your story is consistent. However, it's always a good thing to be honest because somewhere along the lines they might catch up with your lies and that will be considered fraud. Common law and traditional marriages are common; you might get away with such explanations. You cannot get away with lying about a child; everyone knows whether they have a child or not.

It will be of great pleasure if you accept my gratitude because I really need your help on facetime now am going for an f1 student visa to the united states embassy and my interview is around the corner.

All the best I hope you get the Visa kindly watch my embassy videos but overall understand everything you wrote on your DS 160 application. They might ask questions directly from that. Have all your documents., filing fees, passport, photographs, and bank statements. They might not ask for all these things, from experience they are busy dealing with long lines at the embassy, therefore, do a good job on your DS 160 application since that will give them a first impression about you.

We all know the embassy consular are very strict with us and I want to know how to go about it because am a first timer going to further my education. May I also pass greetings from my parent to you. We all take time watching YouTube uploaded video we all love you God bless your hand work.

Thank you so much and pass my greeting to your parents and thank you for watching. With education, you apply for F1 student visa. You need to identify a school that offers your kind of course or degree or something you like. Then visit their website and start an application for international students. They will guide about all you need to submit. After you submit your application and documents, they will decide for admission. If you are admitted they will send to you an I-20 which you will need to submit to the embassy during your interview. The embassy will guide what they need from F1 student applicants. You will need to pay SEVIs fee if they issue an F1 student visa. Good luck.

My daughter has finished campus but no job. Please kindly help how she can get a job in the US.

Congratulations your daughter has completed campus and I am glad you are looking outside the box and coming to American is an option for jobless youth. There are many kinds of visas that your daughter can apply and once she comes here, she will follow other processes that might enable her to find a job. Personally, I recommend student visas because they will give your daughter time to go to school and work as she finds other ways of living and working in the United States permanently.

I have a certificate in nursing, am currently working and the first born of my family. I lost my dad when I was 6 years. My own struggle and my mum's hard work has brought me this far I want to change my life and that of my siblings and family

You have a story to tell and I appreciate you sharing. You need to be a registered nurse 3-4 years training and have nursing license. Once you have these requirements contact nursing agents who will guide you through the process. You will need to pass the American nursing exam called NCLEX and get licensed in one of the 50 states in the United States. The agent will help to find a nursing job that sponsors foreign educated nurses. Through this process, you will get a green card and you can bring your spouse and children if you have them.

Am a registered nurse for two years training but sorry is there any way out?

Apply for registered nurse in a community college or University. You cannot qualify to take the American NCLEX exam if you have less than three years of nursing education.

AI am 35 years old. Are there age limitations when applying for a nursing job in the US via agencies like Avant? Am a BSCN, if I am to come do further studies what courses would I be looking at?

There is no age limit however nursing is physically demanding. You are still young for your information; therefore, no worries there, since you have a bachelor's degree you can apply for master's programs or specialize in any nursing course by taking certification examinations. For example, you might want to get certification in Emergency Room nursing or Intensive Care Unit Nursing. The American Nurses Credentialing Center also known as ANCC offers a variety of certification examinations

Was asking if you know any job opportunity in Canada. Since 1 heard the prime minister of Canada wants 1million immigrants.

The Canadian government gives permanent residency to immigrants from all over the works through a program called express entry which scans qualified candidates according to their education and language abilities in English or French. Those who meet these requirements are invited for further interviews and may obtain jobs in Canada. All these is public information and can be obtained online. However, you must be careful because so many scammers on the internet are taking advantage of these Canadian permanent residency opportunities.

I had appointment at the embassy today as an f-1 student. Unfortunately, I was not granted visa. I wanted to ask was it because I told them I was single because he asked me this same question twice?

Sorry they denied you but there is no way of telling why. Maybe, you did not demonstrate enough ties back home. You need to demonstrate compelling reasons why you will return home. Sometimes the ties can be a good paying stable job, marriage, children, business and much more. Just reapply after 3-6 moths if you think your financial or social situation has changed. Do a good job with your DS 160 application, it should be well detailed to represent your strengths. During the interview be confident and maintain eye contact, sound truthful. Watch my embassy videos, do your best and never give up.

Hi Janet, how are you? I have been talking to a certain guy for probably close to 2 years. We call each other, text, video chat though we have never met. He lives and works in the United States and he is an American citizen. He wants me to visit him and he is willing to send me an invitation letter plus buy me an air ticket. What would your advice and what chances do I have for getting that visa?

if I were you, I would ask him to file fiancée visa its part of knowing each other face to face, the chances of getting denied are higher with Visiting than fiancée in my opinion. If you tell the embassy about visiting your boyfriend, you are simply demonstrating strong ties in the United States. The law tells the embassy to make sure you have strong ties outside the United States before issuing temporary visas. Good luck in case you decide to try the visiting visa, you might be lucky depending on your personal situation. For instance, if you have travelled to the united states or other countries in the past that could work in your favor. Also, if you have strong ties like a well-paying job or an established business that could also be very helpful.

I have the interest to work abroad; specifically, in the sector of primary health care. What are the recommended formalities?? Pls, I need your assistance. Yes, so you must find a way to come over and I discuss those ways in the videos.

It depends on primary care as a medical doctor. Medical doctors are required to take examinations, pass and apply for 3-4 years of medical residency in primary care through the J1 exchange visa. This visa has a 2 years home residency requirement, meaning if the doctor complete residency they are required to go back home to exchange information for 2 years before getting admission back to the United States. Many doctors request immigration to waive the 2-year home residency requirement by working with organizations that have the American interests. When the J1 visa is waived doctors can find jobs mostly in underserved areas where they will be able to apply for green cards.

I'm struggling financially and I won't mind going to Canada or USA to work as I study part time. I'm passionate in nursing and willing to do any job there to make a living. Which visa should I apply, student visa can't work for me, I don't have relatives there but as well I can't mind coming even if it is for six months so that I process papers for my babies? You are so nice to us here; God bless you sister.

Thank you for watching, don't fear student visa, I know it's hard, but it works better than visiting visas. You can try visiting and include the children but when you reach here you will wish for a student visa. Some people come to the United States and change status from visiting visa to green card through asylum if they fear persecution. Some change because of marriage to a United States Citizen. Some change from B visa to student F1 visa. Some chose to move to Canada where it's much easier to get permanent residency. I hope these suggestions are eye openers for you and your children.

My understanding is that the student's visa I must pay for school fees before I come, right??

Not always, some schools may ask for a deposit to secure you a spot, but most school need to verify a bank statement only.

Can I apply for nursing as a form four leaver or any community course?

Yes, to can apply to a community college using your high school transcripts in any field of study including nursing.

Would like to go abroad with my daughter — any best options.

Best options depend on you. So, if you apply for student F1 visa apply for her F2, you may include her in the visiting visa too.

Please help me with any tips or guide; I'm having my visa interview next week. It's a student visa. *Wow, congratulations but the best part should have been to fill the DS 160 very well and detailed before the interview, they might not ask much but watch my embassy videos on YouTube.*

What's the catch for mental health nurses in the United States? *There is no catch you need to be a general registered nurse with a license, find an agent like Adevia, Avant and inter-staff and do NCLEX exams. The agents are well connected with lawyers and nursing facilities that will petition your green card and offer you a nursing job. You don't need a Bachelor of Science degree in nursing a 3-year* *diploma in nursing will be just fine. CGFNS will evaluate your documents and let you know if you qualify.*

I have some immigration issue and I need advice, USCIS is asking me to write reasons why children were not included in the initial visa application. How do I draft it, please advise?

The best would be to find a lawyer; I hope you had good reasons why the children were not included in the initial application because this is not looking good. If you did not make the application yourself, then make sure USCIS knows that and let them know you did not understand the benefits that children can get if that is the truth. Whichever way I wish you good luck.

Hello, I watched your video. If someone lost his confirmation number, he/she can still get it.

What you do is get into the page to check whether selected. Then in place of the confirmation number, there is an option of forgot confirmation number, tap there you will be asked to enter your details and hopefully you will get your confirmation number. Keep your numbers secure next time.

I'm a clinical officer by profession. Is clinical medicine acknowledged in the States?

In the United States, we have Physician Assistants who train using the Medicine model. Generally, they do have a first degree in any field and then go ahead and get a Master's degree in Physician Assistant. You can use your clinical medicine degree to apply to a university then complete the requirements for physician assistants. There is no NLEX equivalent for Clinical officers, A few schools can transition your education in America, but you must go back to school in order to work as a Physician Assistant. The good news you have the brains and will even transition to medicine, nursing, or pharmacy if you are willing to put in the time and money.

Applying for a student visa at my age. I'm 46 years. I've seen you mention that they allow applicants of any age to apply for college. I want to change to be a nurse. Kindly advise where to begin. I'm ready to sponsor myself.

Very good you have the funding to start. The best way is to identify a community college or University that offers nursing and start applying. You do not necessarily have to apply for nursing. You can apply any field of interest using what you already have in terms of education. Once you get admitted to the United States, you can always change and do anything you want. In your case you will do nursing, yes, it is very possible regardless of your age.

Can I apply for the green card lottery from anywhere?

So long you follow directions clearly it does not matter where you apply for the green card. The problem if someone applies for you make sure the application is accurate and submitted only once. Make sure to include your personal email and save the confirmation number.

What about Canada how to apply for lottery and when do they open for applications.

They don't have lottery they use education and skills which you can enter through express entry Canada program. If you get to visit Canada, you might succeed.

My main motivation for wanting to relocate to Canada or the USA is to get access to education and Healthcare for my daughter, who has autism. What is the best approach?

Thank you for sharing your story your daughter is strong. Whichever visa that fits you the most you may apply and include her in the application. For instance, if you apply for F1 student visa include her on F2 visa for spouse and children.

Can a person who has not been to secondary level apply for any visa or is there a way to come over there.

Generally, less educated individuals are disadvantaged when applying for immigration benefits. The truth is the world needs all kinds of skills levels. Yes, it's possible if you apply for a conference in the hotel or hospitality industry because you just never know.

Can you get asylum in America after overstaying your visa?

It's hard to advise once someone who overstays their visa, but some individuals might have a lawyer who is helping with the situation that is beyond my abilities. These days there are waivers that people can use to apply for legal status, but this requires someone to depart the United States and apply from the embassy outside the United States. More about this can be found on USCIS website.

Please can you help me with the step by step process to enable me practice in Us as an RN?

Find a nursing recruiting agency such as Anant health care professions, Adevia and Inter stuff. Work with them because they have connections with lawyers and employers who will file for your immigration benefits and petition for your green cards. If you need to do yourself, you need to start by credential evaluations through CGFNS. Once your credentials are evaluated and you pass something called a visa screen, then you can start applying to do NCLEX from one of the States. Once you pass the NCLEX, the challenge is how will you cross over? Student visa is an option, but you see why I encourage people to use Nursing agents.

HOW TO SUCCESSFULLY MANAGE MONEY AS A NEW AMERICAN

W e all want to make money and use money wisely. We need to start earning and spending money wisely. I believe I am a credible source of information because I have excellent credit myself. My credit is in green, simply the best one can have, over 800 points. My house and my car are basically paid for. I have earned an education that pays me six figures. My experiences and skills can only make me more money going forward. I like talking about what I have achieved and not what I think I can achieve. I share my experiences and my financial journey with you. If you plan on coming to America, and you have this information, I can assure you that having this information will start you on a good note.

Rent or Mortgage Payments

First and foremost, we need to understand the kind of bills to expect while living in the United States so that we are prepared and plan. Rent or Mortgage will more than likely be your biggest bill. Let us start with renting. For starters, rent in America generally depends on the neighborhood. Factors that will affect the market price include demand and supply of the apartments in the area, secure neighborhoods, nice parks, good schools for raising children, easy access to shopping centers and malls just to mention a few. In the United States, be prepared to pay on average 700- 1500 dollars per month on rent alone without considering other bills. Off Couse, this will depend on Geography too, for instance, be prepared to pay more rent in Eastern and Western states compared to Midwestern and Southern states. Off course everything is relative, but this will give a rough idea of what to expect. Additionally, understand that these expensive States also tend to pay their workers more money because of the high living standards. I have explained in detail in previous chapters other common bills to consider. You should be prepared to bring in at least 3000 dollars per month in order to meet your minimum basic needs.

Some people choose to rent, and some choose to buy a house and service mortgages for 5, 10, 15 or 30 years. Short payment period means lower interest rates with high monthly payments. Long payment period means higher interest rates but lower monthly payments. Interest rates are always lower for those with excellent or good credit because creditors and banks trust people high credit scores. What this means is that if you have a high credit score, you are less risky to do business with because you have demonstrated the ability to borrow and pay back consistently. Obviously, if you have low credit scores, you will be less trusted. Going forward, understand that your credit score will speak volumes about your personal integrity. Personally, I have learned from experience not to trust people in the United States that borrow money from me; these people will not pay your money back. The truth is that people with good credit scores do not borrow money from individuals; they should have personal credit cards to borrow from. The fact that they are borrowing money from you means that the banks and creditor do not trust them, why would you trust them? Give such people money you are prepared to lose. Just help them without expectations.

HOW TO ACQUIRE EXCELLENT CREDIT SCORES IN THE UNITED STATES

Some of you will ask about how to build excellent credit. For beginners, you must understand the major credit reporting agencies in the United States that keep a record of your credit scores and report that information to businesses, employers or any other entities wanting to verify your integrity. They compile details about your credit history so potential lenders can use that to determine your lending and borrowing risk. Some examples of Credit Unions are, namely Equifax, TransUnion and Experian.

What this means for you is that any time you conduct business by borrowing and paying back you earn points. Paying back on time is also a good sign that you are a trustworthy individual. On the other hand, if you fail to pay back or always submitting your payment late, those doing business with you will pass that information to credit unions. The goal is to borrow what you can afford and pay back in a timely fashion. Aim always to pay more than what is required per month; this is also known as minimum payments. In other words, you are more likely to pay back more money than you originally borrowed if you keep paying minimum payments. Your goal should always be to clear your credit card debt.

The importance of good credit

The importance of good credit can't be underestimated — maintaining a healthy credit score allows you to focus on wealth-building and setting yourself up for success in the future. General advice is to apply for a credit card early, use that credit card to pay bills and essential items. At the end of each month pay off the credit card using cash money from your debit card. After six months, you will be able to create a credit profile in the United States and lenders will begin to trust you. Continue this process during your entire stay in the United States. Borrow what you can afford. Many banks provide both credit and debit cards, including American Express which is my personal favorite. Most places accept Visa and Master Cards.

You can pay off debt faster

Whether you're hoping to take out an auto loan for a new car or refinance credit card debt into a personal loan, the higher your credit score, the lower your interest rate will be. This means that you'll be able to pay off your loans faster because you'll be paying less interest and more of your payment will go towards the principal balance.

The higher your credit score rating, the less interest you'll have to pay. You can get out of debt many months or even years faster than you previously thought.

You can afford better housing

When it comes to the importance of good credit, you could see a big payoff in your home. As a renter, your landlord may use your credit score as a determining factor of your personal characteristics.

Your credit score is an indicator of whether you pay rent on time, and if you'll be a good tenant. The higher your credit score, the more likely you'll be able to qualify for your ideal apartment. You could also have additional leverage when it comes to negotiating rental terms based on your good history of credit.

If you're in the market to purchase a home, a bank or mortgage company will be looking very closely at your finances. Your credit score is used to determine how big of a home loan you'll be eligible for.

An excellent credit score means qualifying for a lower interest rate on your mortgage, which could mean significant savings over a 30-year term loan, and ultimately being able to afford a bigger and better home.

You can land a better-paying job

Depending on your chosen career field, your credit score could greatly affect your ability to get the job you want. Much like a landlord, some employers view your credit score as evidence of your ability to be responsible, show up to work on time, and be a contributing member of the team.

Up to 47 percent of employers run credit checks on their employees. A poor credit rating could mean less pay, and possibly having to settle for a different position or job altogether.

Your monthly bills will be lower

You may not realize it, but your creditworthiness plays a large part in your monthly household bills. For example, many car insurance companies view your credit history as a direct correlation to the likelihood of whether you'll be in an accident, as well as your ability to make your insurance payments on time.

Utility companies also routinely check credit scores before turning on electricity, water, and gas services to a place of residence. Having a low credit rating could mean that you're required to pay a deposit upfront before being able to use their services.

You can have a better retirement

Establishing a better credit score throughout your adult life will allow you to pay off debt and have more financial freedom. This ultimately enables you to start saving more money towards other goals.

Instead of forking over a lot of money towards interest payments, you'll be able to prioritize financial goals beyond just paying debt, like having a good quality of life during retirement.

WHAT'S THE PRICE TAG FOR A COLLEGE EDUCATION?

C ollege expenses range from tuition to housing to bus passes. See how all these costs add up to a college's "sticker price."

In its most recent survey of college pricing, the College Board reports that a moderate college budget for an in-state public college for the 2017–2018 academic year averaged $25,290. A moderate budget at a private college averaged $50,900. But what goes into these costs?

Tuition

Tuition is what colleges charge for the instruction they provide. Colleges charge tuition by the units that make up an academic year, such as a semester or quarter. Tuition at public colleges is often a bargain for state residents, but not for out-of-staters, who often pay double the tuition of residents.

Tuition can vary by major. Students in the sciences, engineering, computing, premed programs, and the fine arts often pay more. For example, at University of Illinois Urbana-Champaign, students enrolled in the College of Engineering pay up to $5,000 more in tuition than students pursuing other majors.

Fees

Colleges charge fees for services. These fees may include the library, campus transportation, student government, and athletic facilities.

Colleges often report a combined tuition and fees figure. According to the College Board, the average cost of tuition and fees for the 2017–2018 school year was $34,740 at private colleges, $9,970 for state residents at public colleges, and $25,620 for out-of-state residents attending public universities.

Housing and Meals

The cost of "room and board" depends on the campus housing and food plans you choose. The College Board reports that the average cost of room and board in 2017–

2018 ranged from $10,800 at four-year public schools to $12,210 at private schools. Colleges also provide room and board estimates for living off campus based on typical student costs.

Books and School Supplies

Most colleges estimate the average costs for required learning materials. Some colleges even include the cost of a computer and computer accessories. The College Board reports the average cost for books and supplies for the 2017–2018 school year was $1,250 at public colleges and $1,220 at private colleges.

Personal and Transportation Expenses

Colleges may estimate some expenses they don't bill you for. These include local transportation, clothing, personal items, entertainment, etc. The College Board reports that expenses in this category for 2017–2018 ran from $2,730 at private colleges to $3,270 at public universities.

Don't Give Up on a College Because of Its Sticker Price

The price of college may seem overwhelming, but college educations come at many different price levels, and financial aid can greatly reduce your cost. The reported college "cost of attendance" is rarely the cost students pay.

Which Colleges Are the Most Expensive?

Colleges with the highest published prices; Columbia University, University of Chicago and Vassar College are among highly selective four-year institutions. These institutions charge more than $56,000 for their sticker price, but many students pay less than this amount to attend.

"Typically, private liberal arts colleges have the highest sticker price, but that doesn't mean they won't be competitive with other universities given their large endowments – especially if you qualify for financial aid and scholarship opportunities," says Amy Goodman, a principal college admissions counselor at IvyWise, a New York-based admissions consulting company.

Some schools with expensive published prices offer generous financial aid packages. In fact, Brown University, Harvard University and Stanford University, to name a few, meet students' full demonstrated need with no loans added to any financial aid package. While these schools charged more than $50,000 in tuition and fees for the 2018-2019 year, they rank highly among U.S. News' Best Value Schools. This ranking takes account the academic quality and the net cost of attendance for a student who received the average level of need-based financial aid.

Which Colleges Are the Least Expensive?

When it comes to published prices, attending a state school as an in-state student might be the least expensive option. Johnson says that's because "everyone who goes to those schools in effect is getting a scholarship – a discount on the cost of education paid by taxpayers."

He says students who choose to go out of state for college forfeit that subsidy. However, there are few states with tuition reciprocity programs. Minnesota, for example, holds an agreement with several neighboring states – Wisconsin, North Dakota, South Dakota, one institution in Iowa and the Canadian province of Manitoba – that reduces nonresident tuition for Minnesotans to attend their public institutions.

Community College vs. University

If you are wondering whether to attend a community college or a university, you should have a solid understanding of the major differences between the two. Keep reading to get the lowdown so you can make an informed decision about the next step in your education.

As a prospective college student, you probably have an idea of what field you want to enter and perhaps which degree you'll need. Beyond that, though, you may be faced with quite a few choices when it comes to your education. One of the biggest decisions you'll make is choosing between a community college and a university.

Community college used to have a reputation of being less academically serious than traditional four-year universities. But a lot has changed in the world of community college. Most importantly, academic standards have risen, as have the qualifications of the teachers.

The choice of community college vs. university really depends on your overall plan for higher education. There are many benefits to beginning your college career at a community college. The quality of education is comparable to traditional institutions of higher education, tuition is more affordable, and the schedule is more flexible.

Some students are still drawn to four-year universities, which offer many things a community college does not, including campus facilities, sports and a more robust student life. But as you'll see, community colleges are changing the landscape of higher education and offering students many more options in pursuing their degree.

Transferring Credits

Most people attend a two-year community college to fulfill their general education requirements and earn an associate's degree. This includes classes that focus on college- level reading and writing, mathematics, science and social science.

These general credits can then be transferred to a four-year college to earn a bachelor's degree.

Across the country, community colleges have worked to ensure that their associate's degrees match the general education requirements of most universities, especially local ones. For this reason, it has never been easier for students to transfer credits between the two.

Still, you want to make sure your credits will transfer before you begin your community college studies. Talk to an academic advisor and confirm that you're taking the right classes. You need to have a plan beyond the first two years at community college; otherwise you may wind up repeating several classes once you transfer.

Academic Quality

The primary reason that community colleges have grown so much in popularity is because, by and large, they have significantly improved academic standards over the last 15 to 20 years. An associate's degree from a junior college, as they were more commonly called, used to be looked down upon. It was generally assumed-and usually true that academic standards were lower and the classes not as rigorous.

But these days, it is widely accepted that students learn just as much, sometimes more, attending community college. The curriculum is on par with universities, and the classes can be just as challenging. There is still plenty of variety in the industry, but dozens of studies have shown that students transferring from a community college outperform their university counterparts.

One of the main reasons for this level of quality is the faculty. Community colleges now require most professors to have a master's or doctoral degree in their discipline. You may get some younger, less experienced teachers here and there, but there are plenty of seasoned veterans teaching at community colleges.

Many community colleges have reached out to professional industries such as business and science, recruiting career professionals who are actively engaged in their fields and offer unparalleled real-world perspective. Traditional four-year universities typically do not have as much flexibility to do this.

Another big difference is research

If you take your generals at a major research university, you may be attending lots of crowded classes being taught by graduate students. University professors are often more focused on research than teaching.

But community colleges don't have research grants. The professors are hired to teach, and that is where their focus lies. They can give students more attention and often utilize more effective teaching methods. Because of this, many community college students find that the quality of instruction is better, even if the professor hasn't written esteemed books.

Class Size

Another crucial component to the community college experience is small class size. You won't see many huge, crowded lectures if any. Most community college classes have twenty students or fewer. This allows for much more interaction and constructive discussion, rather than a one-sided monologue that is common in lower-level university classes.

The small class sizes also contribute to the quality of the teaching, as described above. Professors in small classes are naturally compelled to make the learning process more engaging and interactive. Classroom discussions are more common, and professors are generally more accessible to students. And with fewer papers and exams to grade, professors can give more feedback and develop personal relationships with students.

Compare this with big public research universities. Many of the general education classes have a similar curriculum to community colleges. But you will be attending plenty of crowded lectures-some containing more than 150 students-that are often taught by graduate students. Of course, there are exceptions to this, but it is a definite trend in universities.

Things get better when you enter your major, but general classes tend to be less intimate and engaging.

Cost of Tuition

Public and private universities are much more expensive; lately the rise in tuition has outpaced average inflation by a wide margin. At a public university, tuition can be upwards of $8,000. It's even higher at private universities. Add on other living expenses and the overall cost, also known as the "sticker price", averages over $20,000.

Across the board, community college is much more affordable. The average tuition is half that of a public university. Part of this is because community colleges are stripped down, avoiding things like big campus infrastructure and extracurricular programs that increase the overhead at large universities.

Books and food still cost as much, but many community college students save money by living at home. Other than this, there won't be a huge difference in your living expenses. But as the cost of tuition keeps rising around the country, more and more people are turning to community college to save money on their first two years of college.

Flexibility

Flexibility is another huge advantage of community college, which are typically designed to cater to students who have jobs or families of their own. The fact that students commute to class, rather than live on campus, also makes it necessary to have built-in flexibility.

If you are raising children or work more than a part-time job, then community college is far and away, the best option for you. The flexibility of the schedule cannot be found in traditional schools. Community colleges offer many more night classes, and, unlike most universities, class attendance is not a requirement. Your level of participation and what you get out of it are up to you.

Student Culture and Campus Life

This is one area where large universities will always have community colleges beat. Most community colleges don't invest as much in campus facilities, athletic programs, and student clubs/organizations. That makes it more affordable, but many students feel the need to have "the college experience", which includes living in student dorms and participating in campus life.

You won't find nearly as much of this culture at community colleges, and certainly no fraternities or sororities. But you may be surprised by some of the campuses in the nation's larger community colleges. Many have invested substantially in campus facilities like student centers, campus dining, computer labs and state-of-the-art classrooms.

Some community college students who transfer to big universities have an adjustment period. It is easy to feel alienated when you're new to an environment and most other people have already been there for two years. Most universities provide services for transfer students that make it easier to engage in the social life of the campus.

If you'd like to play sports but don't feel that you're ready for NCAA Division I competition, you may be able to get more playing time and better enjoy the sport at a community college. Many of the larger schools have active and diverse athletics programs, including competitive football, basketball, track and field, baseball, volleyball and more.

STUDENT FINANCIAL AID IN THE UNITED STATES

S tudent financial aid in the United States is funding that is available exclusively to students attending a post-secondary educational institution in the United States. This funding is to assist in covering the many costs incurred in the pursuit of post-secondary education. Financial aid is available from federal, state, educational institutions, and private agencies (foundations), and can be awarded in the forms of grants, education loans, work-study and scholarships. In order to apply for federal financial aid, students must first complete the Free Application for Federal Student Aid (FAFSA).

International Scholarships

There are many resources available to students to search for scholarships, and there are also many services that charge students for either access to their scholarship database or to conduct a scholarship search on a student's behalf. If you have the time and available resources, most of the scholarship searches can be found online for free. InternationalScholarships.com is one that offers a free scholarship search, and with a little research, you can find many more out there. Take your time, do your homework and you will be able to find all the information you need.

For international students hoping to study in the US, scholarships can be an invaluable help toward financing your goals. Whether you are an incoming first year, a student going on to graduate school, or simply returning to college for a new year, there is financial assistance out there for you.

Ask Your School

No matter where you live or attend school, your first step when searching for scholarships should be your school's financial aid office. Most colleges offer scholarship programs specifically for international students attending the institution. Check out your school's financial aid website or call or email the office if you can't find what you're looking for.

Am I eligible for a scholarship?

Eligibility for a scholarship depends entirely on the scholarship; there is no general rule of thumb on whether you are eligible for a financial award. Some scholarships require students to have a certain TOEFL score; some ask that you are from a certain country; some ask for you to have a certain grade point average. You will need to do your own research to see if you are eligible for a scholarship. It can be confusing but remember that college admissions officers and financial aid experts are there to help you find as much money as you qualify for.

How do I apply?

As with eligibility, there is no set rule on how to apply for scholarships. While some just require you to complete an application form, others may require a specially written piece of work, or for you to be pursuing studies in a certain field. If you find a scholarship for which you think that you may be eligible, contact the award administrator of that award. All the scholarships found in the InternationalStudent.com Scholarship search contain contact details of the award administrator.

JANET RANGI

INTERNATIONAL STUDENT LOANS

Y ou should always carefully evaluate how much money you will need to study in the USA. Then you will need to research and apply for scholarships, financial aid from your school, and find money from any other source, including family funds. After exhausting these avenues, most international students still have a funding gap, and that's where international student loans come in.

Federal student loans are popular with US students studying in the US, but they are not available to international students. Instead, international students are eligible for international student loans, specialized private education loans available to international students studying in the US.

International Student Loans are now a very realistic way to finance your education in the US. Loans are very flexible and can offer loan amounts high enough to pay for your entire education, but with extended repayment terms and reasonable interest rates, so you can afford the repayment after you graduate.

Cosigners

Most international students applying for loans must have a US cosigner in order to apply. A cosigner is legally obligated to repay the loan if the borrower fails to pay. The cosigner must be a permanent US resident with good credit who has lived in the US for the past two years. The cosigner is often a close friend or relative who can assist in getting credit since most international students cannot receive credit on their own. If you're not able to find a cosigner see if there are no cosigner loans available to you.

Repayment

Repayment will vary depending on the loan option you choose. Since most international students are not able to work while they study in the US, repayment must be considered as an extremely important feature in your loan. You will need to consider how much the monthly payments will be when payments will begin, and how long you will be able to defer paying back the loan. The repayment period generally ranges from 10-25 years, but the larger the loan, the longer the repayment period. The standard repayment plan options are:

How Can I Get a Loan Without a Cosigner?

You may be discouraged at how difficult it can be for an international student to find someone to cosign their private loan. Don't be discouraged but focus on those careers that you will easily find employment immediately after graduation. During my research as I was struggling to assist a family member pay for tuition, I came across some companies Stilt, MPOWER and Prodigy Finance. These will offer loans to international students without a cosigner.

JANET RANGI

HOW TO WORK IN THE U.S. WITH A STUDENT VISA

D uring your time as an international student in the U.S., you may decide you want to get a job—whether it's to lighten the load of your tuition, gain some work experience, or just have a little extra pocket money to spend.

Keep in mind, though, that as an international student who is in the U.S. on a visa, you can't just go out and get any job you want. There are regulations you must follow. Working illegally will land you in hot water with the U.S. government. And nobody wants that.

What to Do First

Before you begin the process of finding a job, contact your Designated School Official (DSO). That's the person your school designated to assist international students. If you are already a student, you likely already contacted your DSO when you arrived. But if you haven't, any school official should be able to point you to the right person or department.

Your DSO will help you apply for a Social Security Number (required for all students working in the U.S.) and guide you through the appropriate steps.

Employment Opportunities

The Department of Homeland Security outlines four ways for international students to legally work in the U.S. on an F1 (student) visa:

- On-Campus Employment

- Off-Campus Employment

- Curricular Practical Training (CPT)

- Optional Practical Training (OPT)

On-Campus Employment

On-campus employment is the most freely available to F1 students and refers to work that takes place on campus or at an "educationally affiliated off-campus location."

According to the Department of Homeland Security, being "educationally affiliated" means the off-campus location must meet at least one of these two criteria:

- Associated with the school's established curriculum

- Related to contractually funded research projects at the post-graduate level

- The latter part of that definition is worth emphasizing, as many colleges and universities have buildings and educational partnerships all over town.

So, in other words, you could work somewhere on your school's campus, such as a bookstore, library, dorm, or cafeteria. Or you could work somewhere like an off-campus research lab that is affiliated with your school.

This is the only type of employment you can pursue starting in your first academic year, and you may apply as early as 30 days before classes start.

Work hours are limited to 20 hours per week while school is in session, but you can work full time during holidays and vacation periods. If you choose to work more than one on-campus job, your total combined hours per week cannot exceed 20 hours.

Off-Campus Employment

Jobs outside of your school are only available to international students who have completed one full academic year and who have a qualifying economic hardship or an emergent circumstance.

According to the DHS, a qualifying economic hardship entails "new, unexpected circumstances beyond [your] control," such as:

- Loss of financial aid or on-campus employment (if the student is not at fault)

- Large increases in tuition or living costs

- Substantial decrease in the relative value of currency the student depends upon to pay expenses

- Unexpected changes in the financial conditions for a student's sources of financial support

- Unexpectedly large medical bills not covered by insurance

- Other substantial, unexpected expenses

Emergent circumstances are defined as "world events that affect a specific group of F-1 students and which causes them to suffer severe economic hardship, including, but not limited to natural disasters, wars and military conflicts, national or international financial crises."

Certain regulatory requirements may be suspended for students that are from parts of the world that are experiencing emergent circumstances. This is known as Special Student Relief.

To apply for off-campus employment, contact your Designated School Official (DSO). He or she must approve the reason and recommend off-campus employment as the first part of the application process.

Note that you cannot begin working while your application is still being processed by the Immigration and Customs Enforcement. Apply early so you'll be ready to go when you receive an offer of employment. If approved, you may work 20 hours per week.

Curricular Practical Training (CPT)

Curricular Practical Training (CPT) should be part of your school curriculum. It is designed to give you real-world experience in your field of study, like an internship or practicum with a partnering employer, the DHS explains.

Unlike other employment categories, CPT can be full time, with no weekly hour limit. You can also have more than one CPT authorization at the same time.

Keep in mind that if you participate in a year or more of full-time CPT, you are ineligible for Optional Practical Training, or OPT (which you can read more about below).

To qualify for CPT, you must have completed one full academic year, unless you're a graduate student whose program requires immediate CPT. In any case, the DHS advises seeking your DSO as your first step.

Optional Practical Training (OPT)

Optional Practical Training (OPT) refers to temporary employment relating to your field of study (working at a TV station, for example, would qualify if you're studying journalism). Eligible students can receive up to 12 months of OPT employment.

There are two types of OPT:

- **Pre-completion OPT:** This option is available once you have completed one full academic year at a U.S. college or university. You can work up to 20 hours a week when school is in session or full time when it is not.

- **Post-completion OPT:** You can apply for this option after completing your studies. Those who are authorized for post-completion OPT can work either part time or full time.

You'll need approval from your DSO, who will then endorse your application and help you submit it to U.S. Citizenship and Immigration Services.

Keep in mind that if you participate in both pre-completion and post-completion OPT, the 12-month maximum work period is divided between the two. If you participated in 9 months of pre-completion OPT during your time as a student, you could only participate in 3 months of post-completion OPT after you graduate.

STEM OPT Extension

If you finish your studies and participate in a period of post-completion OPT, you might then qualify for the STEM OPT extension, which is a 24-month period of temporary training that directly relates to your program of study.

This extension is only available if your employer is enrolled in the E-Verify program and if you have a degree in one of the STEMS (science, technology, engineering, or mathematics) fields on this list.

Confused about the difference between Curricular and Optional Practical Training? Check out this helpful cheat sheet!

STEP BY STEP PROCESS OF TRANSITIONING FOREIGN
EDUCATION INTO THE UNITED STATES

TRANSITIONING AS FOREIGN NURSE PROFESSIONAL IN AMERICA

A merica has the largest healthcare budget per person in the world, and one of the reasons for such a large healthcare budget is the need for specialized labor. Specialized healthcare professionals are expensive to train and take a long time to train. This has created a great need for healthcare professionals with the American educational system being incapable of churning out enough professionals to be able to work in the sector. Even if the professionals were trained in the United States, the high cost, the specialized training required would make the cost of healthcare delivery even more expensive to the American citizen.

To plug the gap, the health authorities have resorted to encouraging foreign healthcare professionals to come to America for work to help bridge the gap that is currently being felt in the healthcare industry. Healthcare professionals from middle income and third world nations have thus been moving in droves and migrating to the United States where they are guaranteed of good working conditions and excellent salaries. This has made the United States the largest employer of migrant healthcare workers in the world.

Foreign Educated Health Professionals possess skills that are valuable in America. But it is necessary for a foreign educated nurse to meet the necessary basic training and regulatory requirements to secure an employment opportunity in the health care sector. It is through the following process that I transitioned my foreign nursing credentials.

Transitioning to the American Nursing Workforce requires a detailed process in licensure for foreign educated nurses. This write up will show the necessary steps required for a foreign healthcare professional to transition into the American healthcare sector. The requirements to transition are outlined below.

Attain the educational requirements

To transition smoothly, you will be required to attain educational programs and licenses from your country of origin. This will qualify you to advance your career as a nurse in the American health care setup.

As a foreign Nurse seeking opportunities to live and work in America permanently. You must have;

- Undertaken and graduated from a certified Registered Nursing Program

- Registered and licensed as a Nurse (Registered Nurse)

- At least Two (2) years of clinical practice as a Registered Nurse

Majority of the American States have the mandatory completion of the Foreign Educated Nurses (FEN) course. This is a refresher course will ensure the foreign nurse gets licensed. The course entails 120 hours of clinical practice and 120 hours in the classroom under the direct overseeing or supervision by a registered nurse

Language Proficiency Test

Based on the country of origin, it is highly likely that you will be required to undertake one of the describe tests as outlined below:

- Test of English for International Communication (TOEIC), English as a Foreign Language (TOEFL), or the International English Language Testing System (IELTS).

Recruitment agencies prefer that International clients take either TOEFL or (IELTS).

- The test administration will need to send result of the Foreign Nurse to the state board that they are applying to.

The National Council Licensing Examination-Registered Nurse (NCLEX – RN)

The Foreign Educated Nurse Professional must enroll with the Pearson VUE (Virtual University Enterprises) on a scheduled day and site to take the (NCLEX – RN). You have to exam passed this exam to secure Licensure in the United States. Unlike previously, the NCLEX examination is now offered in multiple countries outside the United States, which is good for nurses looking to work in the United States. Personally, I came as a student, and therefore, I was able to take the NCLEX in the United States.

Seeking an American Based employer or a Recruiting agency

In America, nursing recruiters assist Foreign Educated Nurse Professionals in securing a position as a registered nurse. Nursing recruiters act also act as or serve as US-based employers. Their main role is to assist the Registered Nurse in attaining an immigration Visa. This is inclusive of searching for a job with one of the Health facilities or Hospitals that they collaborate with. I have heard about friends who came through agents such as Avant and Interstaff Health Care professionals. These are just two examples, but there are many other online agents and immigration lawyers who can assist you to navigate the process of coming to the United States as a nurse.

Registered Nurse Immigrant Green Card Visa

To secure an immigrant visa as a Registered Nurse, the following documents are required:

- Supporting evidence is required that you as a Foreign Educated Nurse Professional has the United States based employer acting as your petitioner for your immigrant visa. Nursing recruiters can be your petitioner.

- The Visa Screen Certificate (VSC). This document is given by the International Commission of Health Care (ICHP), a division or agency of the Commission on Graduates of Foreign Nursing Schools (CGFNS).

Visa Interview and Medical Examination

Note that timeline of processing the visa will be based on factors that based on your personal factors such as how fast you respond when documents are required from you. After a successful approval of visa immigration petition

- Your file is sent to the National Visa Center (NVC)for processing by the United States Citizenship and Immigration Service

- NVC forwards the file to the closest US embassy where the visa is issued

- A letter will be sent by the NVC indicating the scheduled date for the visa interview which you will also need to carry with you for official purposes during the interview

- Next will be the medical exam. The letter from the NVC will outline a list of designated physicians that you will contact for the medical process

Registered Nurse Job Offer and Employment Medical Exam

The RN agency/recruiter or employer will have secured a job placement with one of their partner hospitals prior to the visa interview. At this point please provide the RN specialty checklist as well as your résumé. A second medical examination will be required which will be given to the employing hospital. Requirements of the exam vary from hospital to hospital.

Registered Nurse Resuscitation Certification

The following resuscitation certification is required; however, they will depend on the area of practice and guidelines of the hospital.

• Basic Life Support (BLS) certification

• Pediatric Advanced Life Support (PALS) certification

• Advanced Cardiac Life Support (ACLS) certification

You can acquire this certification upon arrival in America. Be certain that the provider of these courses is accredited by the American Heart Association.

JANET RANGI

TRANSITIONING AS A FOREIGN TRAINED DENTIST IN AMERICA

A fter the success of my transition to the United States, I helped others to come to the United States as foreign trained dentists. The process involved passing examinations and going back to University in the United States before they practice dentistry. This was a very insightful experience and formed the basis I have used to mentor others through the system of getting jobs and migrating to the United States. These are some of the procedures the foreign dentist I know personally followed in to start working in the United States. Most of the information is online but through this book, you get first-hand information from those who have lived the process. Keep in mind to apply as many schools as possible. Fees are expensive but if you can demonstrate that you have a close family member or friend willing to co-sign on your loans that will greatly help. Also, go through the Chapter where I wrote about financial aid and getting loans without a cosigner if you have a green card, obviously it's much easier because you will get financial aid for the entire program. If you are denied admission the first time do not quit, this is normal. Make your application stronger by attaining some clinical experiences in the United States, especially in health care or work as a dental assistant. Believe me your personal statement showing your willingness to help people could be the major determining factor whether you get admission or not.

Foreign educated dentists have an opportunity to practice in the United States; they can do so by attending an American Dental Program in the United States. Just to give you real-world examples, the two dentists I know attended University of the Pacific Arthur A. Dugoni School of Dentistry in San Francisco and Loma Linda University in San Bernardino. Both these Schools are found in the state of California, but there several other programs you will find online. Upon graduation and licensure, you can live and work anywhere in the United States. Many dental employers will sponsor your work permit through H1B visa and at which time you may qualify for green card or permanent residency. You may use OPT as you wait for HIB or green card to materialize.

TRANSITIONING AS A FOREIGN TRAINED MEDICAL DOCTOR IN AMERICA

A former professional colleague decided his need for research and technological innovation could not be accommodated outside the United States. When he heard there is a possibility to migrate and become a doctor in the United States, he was thrilled with this possibility. With some help and a very stringent and arduous process, he managed to come to the United States, where he is legally practicing medicine. Through the experiences of my medical doctor friends, I have seen the process they went through to successfully start working and make money as medical doctors in the United States. The trick for foreign doctors is to choose residency programs wisely. Keep in mind that some residency programs are very competitive.

For instance, Orthopedics, Emergency medicine, Dermatology, and Plastic Surgery are very competitive compared to Internal medicine, Family Medicine, Pediatric Medicine, and Psychiatry. If you have a passion for pursuing competitive residency programs, your examination scores and personal statements should be among the best. Remember to use review courses while preparing for examinations. When looking for residency programs, consider applying in rural and underserved areas to lessen the competition. Make sure to apply to as many residency programs as possible.

Consider working in underserved communities and focus on less competitive residency programs to improve your chances of admission. Student loan repayment programs can be available in underserved areas, unlike big cities where programs have more than enough applicants. Make sure to understand the mission statement for each medical program. Another popular option for immigrants is that they get student loan repayments and Citizenship opportunities by serving in the US Military. Many foreign trained medical residents work for the Department of Veteran Affairs (VA), which is a Federal government entity. Working with the government might come in handy if you consider waiving the stringent requirement for J1 visa.

TRANSITIONING AS A FOREIGN PHYSICAL THERAPIST TO AMERICA

The little-known secret is that you can get a green card if you are a qualified Physical Therapist. With a significant number of people in the United States transiting into the elderly bracket, others getting injured and disabled. The need for foreign physiotherapists has really gone up. Through my articles and weekly vlogs, I have recognized people asking how they can come to the United States as physiotherapists, and this prompted my research. The findings have led to the following process log that would be of great help to anyone who would want to come to the United States as a physiotherapist.

As a Foreign Educated Physiotherapist with the desire to work in the United States, your ambition will be determined by a few factors such as the Level of education you have acquired in your country, the process of document evaluation and licensure. These processes are also greatly influenced by the Foreign Credentialing Commission on Physical Therapy.

DON'T TRY TO GET AROUND THE RULES

I f you're considering running your own side gig (like this student who turned his dorm room into a restaurant), know that the U.S. government views that as a job.

To make it legal, you'd have to qualify and apply for OPT, which we covered above.

As you take the next steps toward employment, be mindful that working without adequate authorization can lead to deportation and your inability to return to the United States.

Don't risk it. It's not worth jeopardizing all the effort and expenses you've invested this far. Use the resources available to you, starting with your own school.

JANET RANGI

HOUSING AND ACCOMMODATION: WHAT NEW AMERICANS NEED TO KNOW

I n the USA, it is more common for people to buy their own home than to rent. No matter which of those options you choose, a realtor may help you throughout the process. Finally, no matter if you move to New York or San Francisco, don't forget to set up your utilities in your new home.

There are several destinations in the United States which are, and always have been, popular among immigrants and expats. New York is probably the most famous of them, but San Francisco, Miami, and Chicago also make it to the top ranks.

At the same time, however, there are many downsides to living in these cities, such as the population density and the high rents. It thus makes sense to take a second look at the cities Americans are migrating to and the areas which have a promising economic upswing ahead of them. Smaller cities are always a better option if you want to avoid competition and make more money in your field of study.

Buying vs. Renting

Buying a house or an apartment in the USA is a straight-forward procedure. In general, there are many properties for sale and realtors focus largely on bringing sellers and buyers together. However, this doesn't mean that you do not have to jump some bureaucratic hurdles. As most expats do not have much of credit history in the United States, getting a mortgage is probably the most difficult part. Those who come to the country for a short time only are usually better off renting a home. In some cities, it may be easy to find an affordable house or apartment. In others, you may need strong nerves and a big budget to find a place to live. In any case, you should take a second look at the rental agreement and make sure you understand it before signing it.

Housing and Utilities

One of the places that you will see a lot of variation in the United States is in housing and living accommodations. The average apartment in the United States can run anywhere from $500 (one-bedroom apartments in more rural areas) to $1,500 (3-bedroom apartment in urban areas).

This price could also vary depending on which utilities are included in your rent. Many renters in college towns will include a few utilities in the monthly rent, but that is not always the case. Consult your contract to determine what is included in your rent. Here are some of the most common values you will see for different utilities:

- Electric: $50 to $100 per month, depending on the size of your apartment and if there are energy efficient appliances and lights used. If your heating is electric, it can make your costs up to $150 per month.

- Gas: Not in all apartments. If used for cooking, it will only run from $10 to $15 a month, depending on how much you cook. If used for heating, it can run upwards of $50-$100/month.

- Internet: Averages $45-$50 per month.

- Cellular service: Most services average $50 a month unless you include a data plan, which can push it to upwards of $100 per month.

- Water, sewer, and trash. Many times, this is included in the rent because your landlord will cover it for the entire apartment building. If you do have to pay, however, most municipalities will bill you every quarter (3 months), and it will cost approximately $50-$75 every quarter, depending on the region you reside in.

When you are living in the United States, you will likely want to budget approximately $1000 – $1500 per month for housing and utilities.

Other Costs

Here are some other costs that may come up during your time in the United States. These numbers are just to help you determine how much you may spend

- Groceries for one person, for one week, can run between $20 and $40, depending on what your diet consists of. A gallon of milk costs approximately $3.50, a loaf of bread is about $2.50, Rice is about $1 per pound, and eggs are about $2.00 per dozen. Fresh produce costs quite a bit and will fluctuate depending on which fruits and vegetables are in season.

- Gas costs approximately $3.50 per gallon. If you are lucky enough to be in an area that has public transportation, you can get a monthly pass for approximately $50-$60 (some areas have discounts for students).

- Clothes are relatively expensive unless you go to a large chain department store (Wal-Mart, etc.). A pair of jeans can cost you around $40.

If you are looking for more information about the cost of living in the United States, look at the Number prices for various items; these numbers are based on user input from those who live and/or visit the United States. You can also look at Find the Data, which also does the same sort of user-based input values. The United States Census Bureau puts out relevant information about the cost of living in various areas of the United States.

JANET RANGI

TRANSPORTATION IN THE UNITED STATES

Cost of transportation in the USA

It would be easy to assume that public transportation is cheaper because a bus token is far less expensive than gas, but those are not the only costs to consider. Taking public transportation takes a lot of extra time. You will have to get to the station, possibly in your car where you will have to pay for parking, then get on one or several trains and buses to get to your actual destination. It can easily turn what would have been a 20-minute commute into an hour long one. When it comes to the actual money you would spend on using your car over public transport, public transport is likely going to be cheaper. Passes for the public transportation are somewhere between $20 and $50 a week, depending on where you live. If you must park your car at the station, you can add on another $50 a week at $10 per day. That means that your personal finance would be impacted at about $100 a week, in the city if you drive your car to the station. It drops to less than $50 if you can catch a bus close to home.

If you drive your car, you have a lot of costs to consider. Even if the car is paid off, you are still paying insurance at a rate of $100 a month, if you have a relatively cheap policy. That adds $25 a week. You can also figure a tank of gas a week at an average cost of $2.50/gallon for a 10-gallon tank. That adds another $25 per week.

CREDIT IN THE UNITED STATES WHAT YOU NEED TO KNOW

The importance of good credit

The importance of good credit can't be underestimated — maintaining a healthy credit score allows you to focus on wealth-building and setting yourself up for success in the future. General advice is to apply for a credit card early, use that credit card to pay bills and essential items. At the end of each month, pay off the credit card using cash money from your debit card. After six months, you will be able to create a credit profile in the United States and lenders will begin to trust you. Continue this process during your entire stay in the United States. Borrow what you can afford. Many banks provide both credit and debit cards, including

American Express, which is my personal favorite. Most places accept Visa and Master Cards.

You can pay off debt faster

Whether you're hoping to take out an auto loan for a new car or refinance credit card debt into a personal loan, the higher your credit score, the lower your interest rate will be. This means that you'll be able to pay off your loans faster because you'll be paying less interest and more of your payment will go towards the principal balance.

The higher your credit score rating, the less interest you'll have to pay. You can get out of debt many months or even years faster than you previously thought.

You can afford better housing

When it comes to the importance of good credit, you could see a big payoff in your home. As a renter, your landlord may use your credit score as a determining factor of your personal characteristics.

Your credit score is an indicator of whether you pay rent on time, and if you'll be a good tenant. The higher your credit score, the more likely you'll be able to qualify for your ideal apartment. You could also have additional leverage when it comes to negotiating rental terms based on your good history of credit.

If you're in the market to purchase a home, a bank or mortgage company will be looking very closely at your finances. Your credit score is used to determine how big of a home loan you'll be eligible for.

An excellent credit score means qualifying for a lower interest rate on your mortgage, which could mean significant savings over a 30-year term loan, and ultimately being able to afford a bigger and better home.

You can land a better-paying job

Depending on your chosen career field, your credit score could greatly affect your ability to get the job you want. Much like a landlord, some employers view your credit score as evidence of your ability to be responsible, show up to work on time, and be a contributing member of the team.

Up to 47 percent of employers run credit checks on their employees. A poor credit rating could mean less pay, and possibly having to settle for a different position or job altogether.

Your monthly bills will be lower

You may not realize it, but your creditworthiness plays a large part in your monthly household bills. For example, many car insurance companies view your credit history as a direct correlation to the likelihood of whether you'll be in an accident, as well as your ability to make your insurance payments on time.

Utility companies also routinely check credit scores before turning on electricity, water, and gas services to a place of residence. Having a low credit rating could mean that you're required to pay a deposit upfront before being able to use their services.

You can have a better retirement

Establishing a better credit score throughout your adult life will allow you to pay off debt and have more financial freedom. This ultimately enables you to start saving more money towards other goals.

Instead of forking over a lot of money towards interest payments, you'll be able to prioritize financial goals beyond just paying debt, like having a good quality of life during retirement. What's more, many people reduce costs by downsizing their cars or homes as they enter retirement. Having a strong savings fund will lessen the number of lifestyles changes you make when you stop working.

Don't underestimate the importance of good credit. Proper credit management and smart spending habits will help you.

LEARN MORE ABOUT DIFFERENT OCCUPATIONS AND THEIR REQUIREMENTS

F eedback from my social media platforms and website led me to delve into many other professions apart from the medical field that would enable one to migrate to the United States. The following is a compilation of skilled and semi-skilled labor that is required in the United States and how one can come in as a foreigner and work in the various fields and industries.

Farming, Fishing, and Forestry in The United States

Farming, fishing, and forestry occupations is one of the lowest paid occupational groups, with a median annual wage of \$23,510 compared to the median annual wage for all occupations of \$37,040.

Employment in farming, fishing, and forestry occupations is projected to show little or no change over the next few years. Projected increases in some agricultural worker occupations will be offset by declines in logging occupations.

Agricultural Workers

Agricultural workers maintain crops and tend to livestock. They perform physical labor and operate machinery under the supervision of farmers, ranchers, and other agricultural managers.

Farmers, Ranchers, and Other Agricultural Managers

Farmers, ranchers, and other agricultural managers operate establishments that produce crops, livestock, and dairy products.

Fishing and Hunting Workers

Fishing and hunting workers catch and trap various types of animal life. The fish and wild animals they catch are for human food, animal feed, bait, and other uses.

Forest and Conservation Workers

Forest and conservation workers measure and improve the quality of forests. Under the supervision of foresters and forest and conservation technicians, they develop, maintain, and protect forests.

Logging Workers

Logging workers harvest thousands of acres of forests each year. The timber they harvest provides the raw material for many consumer goods and industrial products.

Additional Farming, Fishing, and Forestry Occupations

Agricultural Inspectors

Agricultural Inspectors inspect agricultural commodities, processing equipment and facilities, and fish and logging operations in order to ensure compliance with regulations and laws governing health, quality, and safety.

Farm Labor Contractors

Farm labor contractors recruit and hire seasonal or temporary agricultural laborers. May transport, house, and provide meals for workers.

First-Line Supervisors of Farming, Fishing, and Forestry Workers

First-Line Supervisors of Farming, Fishing, and Forestry Workers directly supervise and coordinate the activities of agricultural, forestry, aquacultural, and related workers.

Forest and Conservation Technicians

Forest and Conservation Technicians provide technical assistance regarding the conservation of soil, water, forests, or related natural resources.

Graders and Sorters (Agricultural Products)

Graders and Sorters (Agricultural Products) grade, sort, or classify unprocessed food and other agricultural products by size, weight, color, or condition.

Building and maintenance careers

Building maintenance workers can find jobs without formal training, but education and training in areas such as plumbing, dry walling, electrical wiring, and flooring can be helpful when seeking comprehensive 'handymen' jobs. A balanced combination of classroom learning, and hands-on experience gives aspiring maintenance workers the knowledge needed to handle various structural, electrical and HVAC (heating, ventilating and air conditioning) issues that can arise in buildings.

At least some training in basic wiring and plumbing installation and repair is needed for building maintenance jobs. Additional coursework in HVAC systems, mechanical principles, carpentry, refrigeration systems, tool maintenance, and welding is recommended to round out one's knowledge of this field. Classes in mathematics, general construction and safety are also useful. Many of these skills are taught individually within certificate or diploma programs but can be learned collectively in through a degree program.

Licensure requirements for building maintenance professionals vary from state to state and are commonly needed for those working in the specialty areas of plumbing and electrical work. Although not required for employment, a variety of certifications are also available for building maintenance professionals to demonstrate their skill level and maintenance proficiencies. The most widely accepted certifications are offered through the International Maintenance Institute (IMI).

The IMI offers the certified maintenance technician credential at three different levels as well as designations as a certified maintenance professional or certified maintenance manager. IMI certifications are valid for two years and require several continuing education credits for renewal.

As technology advances, so do the computerized control systems installed in newer buildings to control building temperatures, timed lighting schedules, and energy efficiency. Because of this, there is a growing need for building maintenance professionals to develop basic computer skills in order to navigate through computer-controlled equipment. Building maintenance workers should also be able to perform physical tasks, possess manual dexterity, and be able to perform basic mathematical operations.

Building maintenance training programs come in two forms, as building maintenance certificates and facilities management certificates. Through these programs, students can learn various methods for maintaining and repairing the essential systems of a building, as well as prepare themselves for licensure, certification, and additional professional development during their careers.

What General Maintenance and Repair Workers Do

General maintenance and repair workers fix and maintain machines, mechanical equipment, and buildings. They paint, repair flooring, and work on plumbing, electrical, and air-conditioning and heating systems, among other tasks.

General maintenance and repair workers often carry out many different tasks in a single day. They could work at any number of indoor or outdoor locations. They may work inside a single building, such as a hotel or hospital, or be responsible for the maintenance of many buildings, such as those in an apartment complex or on a college campus.

Jobs in this occupation typically require a high school diploma or equivalent. General maintenance and repair workers often learn their skills on the job for several years. They start outperforming simple tasks while watching and learning from skilled maintenance workers.

The median annual wage for general maintenance and repair workers was $37,670 in May 2017.

Construction

Individuals who are interested in becoming contractors often learn the skills of the trade through hands-on training and working on a construction site. Before becoming a contractor, many people have a job as a laborer. Apprenticeships and internships provide valuable training in carpentry, plumbing, electrical work or masonry, and can sometimes substitute for an education background.

It is more common to have a bachelor's degree to work as a contractor, and many accredited colleges and universities offer programs in construction science, construction management, building science or civil engineering, according to the U.S. Bureau of Labor Statistics (BLS) (www.bls.gov). These programs focus on various aspects of the construction business, including classes in site planning, designing, construction methods, contract administration, building codes and standards, as well as mathematics, accounting, and information technology.

Master's degree programs are also available at many institutions in construction management or construction science. Some construction professionals seek out bachelor's or master's degrees in business administration or finance as well. Those with master's degrees in this field often become contractors at larger construction or construction management companies due to their credentials, as reported by the BLS.

While certification is not required to work in construction management, it is becoming more common because it shows competence and demonstrates the proper training in the field. Certification opportunities are available at the American Institute of Constructors and the Construction Management Association of America, according to the BLS.

The American Institute of Constructors offers the Associate Constructor (AC) and Certified Professional Constructor (CPC) designations to those who meet the requirements and successfully complete the proper examinations. The Construction Management Association of America awards the Certified Construction Manager (CCM) designation to workers who have the required experience and pass a technical examination.

Applicants can improve their ability to compete for jobs by completing a bachelor's degree in construction management or construction science and acquiring a state license.

Most employers require construction and building inspectors to have at least a high school diploma and work experience in construction trades. Inspectors also typically learn on the job. Many states and local jurisdictions require some type of license or certification.

The median annual wage for construction and building inspectors was $59,090 in May 2017. $28.41 per hour

Production

A career as in manufacturing can be pursued with a high school diploma or GED. Experience using tools is typically required, and those who enter this field will have to complete workplace safety courses and other training through their employer.

The manufacturing industry is a diversified field that includes jobs ranging from production workers to purchasing agents. The top two occupations in manufacturing are team assemblers and machinists. The third most populous occupation, which may be thought of as quality control employees, includes inspectors, testers, sorters, samplers and weighers.

Required Education High school diploma or GED

Other Requirements On-the-job training and voluntary certifications available

Median Salary $40,550 annually for machinists

Source: *U.S. Bureau of Labor Statistics

Manufacturing Career Options

Team assemblers

Team assemblers fabricate or construct products on an assembly line. In order to respond to demand shifts, these workers rotate on different assignments throughout the production process. By doing this, they become well-versed in all stages of assembly and can adjust to worker absences and supply chain issues. Team assemblers may also be responsible for quickly scanning parts, removing faulty parts and determining the source of a defect.

As reported by the U.S. Bureau of Labor Statistics (BLS), employment growth for assemblers and fabricators is projected to decline one percent from 2014 to 2024. This job decline is due to an increase in productivity with fewer workers in many manufacturing companies. In May 2015, the BLS stated that team assemblers earned a median annual salary of $29,080.

Machinists

Machinists use specialized tools, including computer numerically controlled (CNC) machines, to create or assemble parts, mechanisms, and products. Machinists begin by consulting blueprints or instructional guides to determine the equipment to use and actions to take. These professionals then perform the required work and follow-up by inspecting products for structural integrity and accuracy to specifications.

Machinists could see ten percent of employment growth between 2014 and 2024, according to the BLS. A continuing need for machinists despite advances in technologies is expected. As of May 2015, the BLS says, machinists earned a median yearly salary of $40,550.

Inspectors, Testers, Sorters, Samplers, and Weighers

This group ensures quality control by checking products for specification and functional conformance. This may include verifying weights and measures, as well as testing and sending back defects. Additional duties may include reviewing products for durability and fixing minor problems.

The BLS indicates that as of May 2015, 508,590 employed inspectors, testers, sorters, samplers, and weighers earned a median annual salary of $36,000. Employment for quality control inspectors, which includes those that inspect manufacturing equipment and products, is expected to see no job growth during the 2014-2024 decade.

Requirements

Prospective candidates may enter the manufacturing field after completing high school. These new hires may receive on-the-job training on handling power tools, assembling parts and using specific quality-control instruments to verify dimensions. Additionally, new employees may participate in employer-sponsored classroom assignments on topics ranging from occupational safety to assembly line controls.

Some positions may ask for postsecondary education. For example, inspectors may benefit from having earned a certificate in computer-aided design. These 6-12-month programs may include instruction on design setup, scaling and modification. Similarly, machinists may be required to have completed a 2-year associate's degree program or 4-year apprenticeship. Apprentices may receive training on reading mechanical drawings, setting up equipment and operating specialized machinery, such as CNC machines.

Sales

Rewarding sales careers are found in just about every industry. Employees realize a strong sales team often leads to a successful company. Many companies make hiring skilled sales professionals a top priority.

Many professionals choose a sales career for personal satisfaction, freedom from the office, growth and high-income potential. Salespeople are paid for their performance.

Hard work and a successful sale record often lead to a promotion such as gaining more prestigious customers, a sales executive trainer position or a sales manager job.

Many of the high paying sales jobs require a higher level of knowledge. Salespeople in the low earning sales jobs typically sell a product, whereas salespeople in the high earning sales positions typically sell a solution.

Sales careers often require appropriate education, training, experience, knowledge as well as good interpersonal skills. Some sales jobs involving scientific and technical products require a bachelor degree. However, some sales jobs don't require post-secondary education.

Many companies require beginning sales representatives to participate in a formal training program which can take up to two years to complete.

Different Sales Careers:

• Advertising Sales Agents

• Insurance Sales Agents

• Real Estate Brokers and Sales Agents

- Sales Engineers

- Securities, Commodities and Financial Services Sales Agents

- Travel Agents

- Wholesale and Manufacturing Sales Representatives

Advertising Sales Agents

An advertising sales agent career can technically begin with a high school diploma or proven sales experience; however, some employers prefer applicants with a bachelor degree in Marketing, Communication, Business, or Advertising. Most advertising sales agents receive on-the-job training.

Insurance Sales Agents

People interested in an insurance sales agent career typically need at least a high school diploma, although a growing number of agents now have a Bachelor of Business, Economics, Finance, or a related degree. Upon hire, insurance sales agents typically shadow an experienced insurance sales agent to receive on-the-job training.

Insurance sales agents need to have a license in every state they work. Agents selling life and health insurance and property and casualty insurance must obtain separate licenses.

Most state licenses require the insurance sales agent to take continuing education courses every two years.

Insurance sales agents may obtain voluntary certifications demonstrating expertise in specific areas.

Some insurance sales agents opt to become certified to sell additional financial planning services in order to meet consumer demand. Insurance sales agents can obtain these additional certifications through the National Association of Securities Dealers (NASD) which includes the Series 6 exam (for selling only mutual funds and variable annuities), and the Series 7 exam, which qualifies the individual as a general securities sales' representative.

Insurance sales agents must know their product inside out, as they must clearly explain it to potential customers, knowledgeably answer any questions, and make helpful suggestions as to which policy to select or any policy changes a customer should make. An Insurance sales agent career includes helping customers with the claim process.

Insurance sales representatives may advance in their career to a managerial position after obtaining experience and perhaps additional education.

Essential Career Information

Education requirement: High school diploma or equivalent

2017 median pay $49,710

(source: Bureau of labor statistics)

Food and beverages

Many food preparation jobs are entry-level jobs in the culinary industry; however, some jobs are at a higher level. Typically, people don't need a degree to enter the food preparation industry, however, professionals seeking a food preparation career may benefit from completing a culinary program.

Food preparation employees take care of routine tasks such as slicing vegetables, slicing meats and measuring ingredients. Food preparation workers also make sure they work in a clean environment.

Many employers seek food preparation workers with at least a high school diploma. Most food preparation workers receive on-the-job training.

Quick facts regarding food and beverages and other related workers

2017 Median Pay: $20,410 per year

$9.81 per hour

Typical Entry-Level Education: No formal educational credential

Work Experience in a Related Occupation: None

On-the-job Training: Short-term on-the-job training

Food and beverages careers

- Bartenders

- Chefs and Head Cooks

- Food Service Managers

Bartenders

Typically, to enter a bartender career, workers need to be 18 and older and complete short-term on-the-job training. There are no educational requirements required for a bartender career. However, people who desire to work at higher end restaurants or establishments need more experience and some vocational training.

Training programs include teaching bartenders about customer service, cocktail recipes, state and local laws, how to deal with difficult or unruly patrons, teamwork and proper food procedures.

Chefs and Head Cooks

Typically, people need a high school diploma, formal training from a technical, culinary arts school or community college, and experience to enter a head cook career. Some chefs learn skills through apprenticeships or in the armed forces.

Culinary programs and vocational schools offer classes under experienced chefs in areas including food sanitation procedures, kitchen work, menu planning, and purchasing/inventory methods. Many programs require head cooks to gain real-world kitchen experience through apprenticeships. Associations such as culinary institutes, and trade unions and the U.S. Department of Labor sponsor apprenticeships; they typically last for about two years.

Food Service Managers

Individuals typically do not need a college degree to begin a food service management career. However, increasingly, employers seek candidates with some postsecondary education and training. Many food service management companies and national restaurant chains recruit at college hospitality and food management programs. Technical schools and community colleges provide training for individuals interested in a food service manager career.

Most certification and degree programs offer work-study training as well as classes in areas such as nutrition and food preparation, business management and computer science. In addition, restaurant chains and food management companies, such as healthcare food service management, offer intensive training programs. These programs include food preparation, nutrition, employee management, and education on company procedures.

Food services managers don't need certification; however, the National Restaurant Association Educational Foundation offers the Foodservice Management Professional (FMP) certificate to recognize outstanding professional service of food service managers.

Mathematics and computing

Rewarding mathematics jobs are available in an array of companies and organizations. A postsecondary education in mathematics provides a variety of career paths. Most math careers go far beyond just crunching numbers, they're challenging, interesting and provide a good salary.

Some careers focus on mathematical research and education, whereas others use mathematics and its applications to build and improve work in finance, sciences, manufacturing, business, engineering and communications. Some mathematicians work in fields such as climate study, astronomy and space exploration, national security, medicine, animated films and robotics.

The Federal Government, mainly in the U.S. Department of Defense, employs many mathematicians. Some working for the Federal Government work for the National Institute of Standards and Technology or the National Aeronautics and Space Administration.

Mathematics Careers:

- Actuaries

- Mathematicians

- Operations Research Analysts

- Statisticians

Actuaries

People interested in an actuarial career typically need at least a Bachelor of Mathematics, Bachelor of Statistics, Bachelor of Business, or Bachelor of Actuarial Science degree. Many actuarial students obtain an internship while in school.

Actuaries must pass multiple exams to become certified actuarial professionals; many employers expect actuaries to have passed at least one of these exams prior to graduating with their bachelor degree.

The Casualty Actuarial Society (CAS) and the Society of Actuaries (SOA) both offer two levels of certification: associate and fellowship

Certification through the SOA requires passing a series of five exams, plus seminars on professionalism.

Certification through the CAS requires passing a series of seven exams, plus seminars on professionalism.

Actuaries working in the property and casualty field become certified through the CAS, while actuaries working in the life insurance, health insurance, retirement benefits, investments, and finance receive certification through the SOA. Certification through either society takes four to six years. It generally takes actuaries two to three years to continue and earn fellowship status.

Essential Career Information

Median Pay$93,680

Entry-level education requirements Bachelor's degree

(source: Bureau of Labor and statistics)

Mathematicians

An entry-level position in a mathematician career requires at least a Bachelor of Mathematics or significant coursework in mathematics. Employers prefer candidates who double majored in mathematics and a related field such as computer science, engineering, or physical science.

In the private industry, mathematicians typically need a minimum of a Master of Applied Mathematics or Master of Theoretical Mathematics. Mathematicians don't need specific certifications or licenses.

Essential Career Information

Median Pay $101,360

Entry-level education requirements Master's degree

(source: Bureau of labor statistics)

Operations Research Analysts

An operations research analyst career begins with a minimum of a Bachelor of Operations Research degree, a Bachelor of Management Science degree, a Bachelor in Mathematical

Sciences or a bachelor's degree in a related field such as engineering, physics, mathematics, or computer science.

Most operations research analyst jobs beyond an entry-level job require a master's degree, such as a Master's degree in Operations Research or a Master's degree in Management Science.

Operations research analysts don't need specific licenses or certification; however, taking continuing education courses throughout their career helps them keep up with technology advances.

Essential Career Information

Median Pay$72,100

Entry-level education requirements Bachelor's degree

(source: Bureau of Labor Statistics)

Statisticians

A statistician career typically begins with a Master of Statistics, Master of Mathematics, or Master of Survey Methodology degree. Occasionally, a statistician may obtain an entry-level position with a bachelor degree, but a master's degree is increasingly the standard. Research and academic statistician jobs usually require a Ph.D. No specific certification or license is required for statisticians.

Essential Career Information

Median Pay$75,560

Entry-level education requirements Master's degree

Life, Physical, and Social Sciences

The life, physical and social sciences sectors provide a wide variety of interesting careers. The sectors provide administrative, management, technician and research jobs.

Many of the life, physical and social sciences careers require at least a bachelor degree, however many of the careers require a graduate degree, specific training and experience. In the life sciences, sector over 50 percent of medical and other life scientists have a doctoral degree.

Most scientists work in the private sector; about 27 percent of scientists work for federal, state and local government agencies.

Life sciences careers typically involve study living organisms. Physical science careers typically involve the study and application of the principles of chemistry and physics.

Professionals with social sciences careers examine human society and relationships of individuals. Social sciences careers may involve performing research or other professional or scientific work in one field or a combination of social sciences fields. The social sciences sector also includes a variety of administrative and management positions.

Life, Physical, and Social Sciences Careers:

- Agricultural and Food Science Technicians

- Agricultural and Food Scientists

- Anthropologists and Archeologists

- Atmospheric Scientists and Meteorologists

- Biochemists and Biophysicists

- Chemical Technicians

- Chemists and Materials Scientists

- Conservation Scientists and Foresters

- Economists

- Environmental Science and Protection Technicians

- Environmental Scientists and Specialists

- Epidemiologists

- Forensic Science Technicians

- Forest and Conservation Technicians

- Geographers

- Geological and Petroleum Technicians

- Geoscientists

- Historians

- Hydrologists

- Medical Scientists

- Microbiologists

- Natural Sciences Managers

- Nuclear Technicians

- Physicists and Astronomers

- Political Scientists

- Psychologists

- Sociologists

- Survey Researchers

- Urban and Regional Planners

- Zoologists and Wildlife Biologists

Agricultural and Food Science Technicians

Agricultural and food science technologists generally need an Associate in Animal Science degree or an Associate in Food Science degree or an associate's degree in a related field. Some schools offer an Associate in Agricultural Technology Food Science degree.

Many schools offer internships, cooperative education and other experiential programs for food technologists.

People who choose food science careers and have only a high school diploma usually undertaken an extensive training program that can last a year or more.

Essential Career Information

Median Pay$34,070

Entry-level education requirements Associate's degree

Agricultural and Food Scientists

People need at least a bachelor's degree in agricultural science, biology, chemistry or physics to begin an agricultural science career or a food scientist career. Botany, chemistry and plant conservation degrees provide good preparation for soil and plant science work.

Organizations such as the American Registry of Professional Animal Scientists certify agricultural scientists and food scientists recognized for expertise in this field. While not required, the agriculture and food science industry recognize the value of certification. Some states do require licensing for soil scientists.

Essential Career Information

Median Pay$58,070

Entry-level education requirements Bachelor's degree

Anthropologists and Archeologists

Candidates need a master's degree to pursue an anthropology career or an archeology career. Leadership roles and jobs requiring more technical expertise may necessitate a doctoral degree; especially true when it comes to anthropology or archeology projects outside the country. Those who have a bachelor's degree may find lab or fieldwork.

Many colleges and universities offer a Master in Cultural Anthropology degree, a Master in Physical Anthropology, a Ph.D. in Anthropology or a graduate forensic anthropology program.

Essential Career Information

Median Pay$57,420

Entry-level education requirements Master's degree

Personal Care and Service

The personal care and services sectors include a variety of careers and many workers. Personal care and services careers attract people who enjoy being involved with other people throughout the workday.

Some of the personal care and services jobs require a state license. Some schools provide specialized education programs for people interested in personal care and services careers. The length of these education programs ranges from several weeks to two years.

Personal Care Careers:

- Animal Care & Service Workers

- Barbers, Hairdressers & Cosmetologists

- Childcare Workers

- Fitness Trainers & Instructors

- Funeral Directors

- Gaming Services Workers

- Home Health Aides & Personal Care Aides

- Manicurists & Pedicurists

- Massage Therapists

- Recreation Workers

- Skincare Specialists

- Travel Agents

Animal Care and Service Workers

People interested in an animal care worker career or an animal service worker career, frequently learn on-the-job, but many employers require candidates to have a high school diploma. Some community college and vocational programs serve people who want to train dogs or horses.

In some cases, a college degree helps; zoos typically seek animal care technicians with a bachelor's degree in biology, animal science or a similar field.

Animal care workers seeking to serve as pet groomers have the option of attending a state-licensed grooming school.

Animal care workers who choose to work at a marina may need a bachelor's degree in marine biology, animal science or a related field.

Essential Career Information

Median Pay$20,840

Entry-level education requirements None

Barbers, Hairdressers and Cosmetologists

Those who choose a barber career, a hairdresser career or a cosmetologist career need a high school diploma or equivalent and complete a state-licensed program in hairstyling, skin care or similar area. High schools and vocational schools offer barber, hairdresser and cosmetology courses, sometimes leading to an associate's degree. Those who work solely as shampooers need no formal education. All barbers, hairstylists and cosmetologists must pass a state licensing exam.

Essential Career Information

Median Pay$22,700

Entry-level education requirements Vocational training

Childcare Workers

Requirements for people seeking a childcare worker career vary among states, employers, and the goals of the job. Some states require those who choose a childcare career to have a high school diploma, and many require daycare providers and family childcare providers to have a license.

Becoming a licensed center or daycare provider involves staff background checks, complete immunization records, and a minimum training requirement.

While some states have no requirements for childcare workers, some employers require an associate's degree in early childhood education or a child development credential.

States often require daycare workers to have Child Development Associate certification through the Council for Professional Recognition. The certification requires coursework, experience, and a high school diploma. Median Pay$19,510.

Fitness Trainers and Instructors

Educational requirements for those who choose a fitness trainer career or fitness instructor career depend on the specialty involved. Many employers prefer to hire certified fitness trainers. Personal fitness trainer, group fitness instructor, and specialized fitness instructor require different skills.

Some employers seek applicants with a bachelor's degree in physical education, physical fitness or exercise science.

People seeking a personal trainer career often need certification to work with clients or members of gyms or health clubs. Most fitness trainers or fitness instructors need

CPR certification before getting their physical fitness certification. Basic certification requires no specific training or education; however, fitness trainers and fitness instructors can take exams, workshops and seminars.

Essential Career Information

Median Pay$31,720

Entry-level education requirements High school diploma or equivalent

Health care support

The thriving healthcare field offers some of the nation's best career opportunities. If you're seeking a personally and financially rewarding career, consider the healthcare industry. Well-paid healthcare professionals work with caring co-workers to improve peoples' lives.

Due to the increasing larger elderly population, the demand for healthcare and medical professionals continues to increase. The healthcare and medical sectors encompass an array of rewarding careers. The health/medical industry continually seeks qualified professionals for a variety of healthcare careers and medical careers.

Many healthcare careers only require a two-year degree or a certificate. Many of the health careers and medical careers require people to complete a licensure program or course training. Many of the careers in health and medical technology require specific certifications.

Medical Careers:

- Cardiovascular Technologists and Technicians and Vascular Technologists

- Diagnostic Medical Sonographers

- EMTs and Paramedics

- Home Health Aides and Personal Care Aides

- Licensed Practical Nurses (LPNs) and Licensed Vocational Nurses (LVNs)

- Medical and Clinical Laboratory Technologists and Technicians

- Medical and Health Services Managers

- Medical Appliance Technicians

- Medical Assistants

- Medical Equipment Repairers

- Medical Records and Health Information Technicians

- Medical Scientists

- Medical Transcriptionists

- Nursing Aides, Orderlies, and Attendants

- Physician Assistants

- Physicians and Surgeons

- Psychiatric Technicians and Psychiatric Aides

- Radiation Therapists

- Radiologic Technologists

- Registered Nurses

Cardiovascular Technologists and Technicians and Vascular Technologists

People interested in a cardiovascular technologist, cardiovascular technician or vascular technician career generally need an Associate of Radiologic Technology degree or an Associate of Nursing degree. However, some cardiovascular technologists have a Bachelor of Radiologic Technology degree.

In most programs, associates or bachelors, students work with experienced technologists or technician in a lab setting for course credit. Some schools provide an Associate in Cardiovascular Sonography degree.

Some community colleges offer one-year certifications for individuals who have already received training in a medical field.

A cardiovascular technician working as an EKG technician usually receives 4-6 weeks of on-the-job training from their employer.

Cardiovascular technologists, cardiovascular technicians, and vascular technicians do not require certification, but it's highly recommended, as most employers prefer certification. Many insurance providers only pay for work conducted by a certified cardiovascular technologist, a certified cardiovascular technician, or a certified vascular technician.

A variety of certifications for cardiovascular technologists, cardiovascular technicians, or vascular technicians exist, depending on their clinical focus, and they may become certified in multiple areas. In most cases, cardiovascular technologists, cardiovascular technicians, or vascular technicians must take continuing education courses to maintain their certification.

Essential Career Information

Median Pay$52,070

Entry-level education requirements Associate's degree

Diagnostic Medical Sonographers

Individuals seeking a diagnostic medical sonographer career typically need an Associate of Sonography or a postsecondary certificate from an accredited institute or hospital program. Colleges offer an Associate in Sonography degree and a Bachelor in Sonography degree. Some colleges offer an Associate in Cardiovascular Sonography degree program or an Associate in Diagnostic Medical Sonography degree program.

Individuals already involved in the healthcare field can obtain a one-year certificate. Some sonographers obtain a degree in radiologic technology or nursing, then receiving on–the-job training.

Many employers prefer or even require a professional certification. Certification involves graduating from an accredited program and passing an exam related to the specialty the diagnostic medial sonographer is most interested in. Diagnostic medical sonographers must also take continuing education courses to keep their certification up to date.

Some states also require licensure for diagnostic medical sonographers. Requirements for licensure vary by state.

Essential Career Information

Median Pay$65,860

Entry-level education requirements

* Associate's degree

EMTs and Paramedics

Individuals interested in an EMT career or a paramedic career need to have a high school diploma, or equivalent, cardiopulmonary resuscitation (CPR) certification, and a state license.

People interested in an EMT career or a paramedic career can obtain formal training from technical institutes, community colleges, and other facilities specializing in emergency care training.

EMT-Basics have the least amount of training, while paramedics have the most amount of training. Paramedics may obtain their training through a community college, earning an associate's degree.

EMTs and paramedics must take a course and become certified to drive an ambulance.

EMTs and paramedics may be certified by the National Registry of Emergency Medical Technicians (NREMT) on four different levels: EMT-Basic, EMT-Intermediate 1985, EMT-Intermediate 1999, and Paramedic. Some states have their own certification and may use different titles for the same positions.

EMTs and paramedics must obtain a state license; the requirements vary by state.

Essential Career Information

Median Pay$31,020

Entry-level education requirements

• Post-secondary non-degree award

Home Health Aides and Personal Care Aides

Most home health care aides and personal care aides have a high school diploma, although no specific education requirements exist for this position. Home health aides and personal care aides typically receive on-the-job training. Some employers may require a competency evaluation prior to hiring.

Some states have no training requirement for home health aides and personal care aides, but other states require a formal training from a community college, vocational school, elder care program, or home health care agency. Some states also require a background check for all home health aides and personal care aides.

Home health care aides working for an employer receiving reimbursements from Medicare or Medicaid must obtain training and pass a competency evaluation or earn state certification.

Home health aides and personal care aides may receive certification from the National Association for Home Care and Hospice (NAHC). Certification is not required, but many employers prefer to hire certified workers.

Essential Career Information

Median Pay$19,910

Entry-level education requirements: Less than high school

Transportation Careers

More than eight million Americans have transportation jobs, including over three million truck drivers who transport raw materials and products throughout the nation. A growing population increases the demand for products which creates growth in the transportation industry.

Some transportation careers require postsecondary education, whereas other transportation careers require training obtained through a trade school or on-the-job training. Transportation careers such as pilot, air traffic controller, and postal worker require extensive, specialized training.

The transportation industry also includes clerical and management jobs. Typically, a transportation manager oversees all transportation services for a company.

Transportation Careers:

- Automotive Service Technicians and Mechanics

- Bus Drivers

- Cargo and Freight Agents

- Delivery Truck Drivers and Driver/Sales Workers

- Diesel Service Technicians and Mechanics

- Heavy and Tractor-Trailer Truck Drivers

- Heavy Vehicle and Mobile Equipment Service Technicians

- Material Moving Machine Operators

Automotive Service Technicians and Mechanics

A vocational or postsecondary training program in automotive service technology is the new standard for automotive technician and automotive mechanic entry-level jobs. Automotive service technology programs typically last six months to one year, although some schools offer a two-year Associate in Automotive Service Technology degree program. Automotive manufacturers and dealers sponsor many of the associate's degree programs.

An automotive service technician career typically begins with on-the-job training, working under the instruction of an experienced technician for two to five years before being considered a fully qualified service technician. Automotive service technicians generally work another one to two years before becoming familiar with all types of repairs.

Automotive service technicians working with refrigerant are required by the U.S. Environmental Protection Agency to obtain a license in proper refrigerant handling.

Most employers require automotive service technicians to become certified from the National Institute of Automotive Service Excellence. Automotive service technicians can become certified in any of the following: automatic transmission/transaxle, brakes, electrical/electronic systems, engine performance, engine repair, heating and air conditioning, manual drive train, and axles, or suspension and steering. A Master Automotive Technician has certification in all eight areas.

The Certified Professional Manufacturers' Representative (CPMR) certification or the Certified Sales Professional (CSP) demonstrates industry credibility.

Essential Career Information

Median Pay$36,610

Entry-level education requirements High school diploma or equivalent

Bus Drivers

People interested in a bus driver career, typically need a commercial driver's license (CDL) and training, and they must meet hearing and vision test standards. Training consists of one to three months practicing bus maneuvers and light traffic driving that leads to practice runs on specific routes. Experienced bus drivers accompany the new trainees and provide performance evaluations.

Bus drivers need to pass a written test and a driving test to obtain a commercial driver's license (CDL). Bus drivers may also need special endorsements to drive a school or passenger bus. People need to pass knowledge and driving tests to obtain a school (S) endorsement or a passenger (P) endorsement. Bus drivers also must pass random drug and alcohol tests during their bus driver career.

Essential Career Information

Median Pay$36,600

Entry-level education requirements High school diploma or equivalent

Cargo and Freight Agents

Typically, people interested in a freight career need a high school diploma or a GED and on-the-job training. As training progresses, cargo agents take on more complex jobs such as notifying customers of shipment times and deliveries as well as monitoring shipments en route.

Cargo and freight agents use specific shipment software programs and computer databases which require a short time of computer training.

Essential Career Information

Median Pay$39,720

Employment growth forecast, 2010-202029 percent

Entry-level education requirements High school diploma or equivalent

Delivery Truck Drivers and Driver/Sales Workers

People interested in a delivery truck driver career or a driver/sales worker career need a high school diploma or equivalent and a state issued driver's license and undergo less than one month of training on the job. The training typically includes working with an experienced driver who rides along with a new worker to make sure that he/she can operate and handle a truck in difficult road conditions. In addition, drivers may also take classes from their employer to learn policies and procedures.

Median Pay$22,670

Engineering and Architecture

Most architects get their training through a five-year bachelor of an architecture degree program; some earn a master's such as a Master of Architecture, which can take one to five years depending on previous education and experience.

All states require architects to obtain a license, which can include a professional degree in architecture, practical training and internship. An architect must also pass the Architect Registration Examination. Most states require continuing education to maintain licensure.

Engineering, a broad field, includes an array of rewarding specialties; most engineers specialize in an area. Qualified engineers are in demand in a variety of fields.

Typically, engineers need math and science knowledge. People seeking an engineering career typically need a bachelor degree in engineering or a relevant field. Some engineering jobs, especially in management, require a master's degree. An engineering degree in a specialty area may qualify engineers for an engineering career in another applicable area.

Many engineers have rewarding careers working on cutting edge technology. Many engineering jobs involve computers. Due to the engineering sector relying on continual innovation, the best engineers enjoy a changing work environment. Engineers often work as a team to come up with new innovations.

A study performed by the U.S. Department of Labor shows professional engineers tend to stay employed with the same company for significantly longer periods of time than workers in other professions.

Engineering Careers:

- Aerospace Engineering and Operations Technicians

- Aerospace Engineers

- Agricultural Engineers

- Biomedical Engineers

- Cartographers and Photogrammetrists

- Chemical Engineers

- Civil Engineering Technicians

- Civil Engineers

- Electrical and Electronic Engineering Technicians

- Electrical and Electronics Engineers

- Electro-Mechanical Technicians

- Engineering Managers

- Environmental Engineers

- Health and Safety Engineers

- Industrial Engineering Technicians

- Marine Engineers and Naval Architects

- Materials Engineers

- Mechanical Engineering Technicians

- Mechanical Engineers

- Mining and Geological Engineers

- Nuclear Engineers

- Petroleum Engineers

- Sales Engineers

- Surveying and Mapping Technicians

- Surveyors

Aerospace Engineering and Operations Technicians

Candidates for avionics technicians' jobs should be detail-oriented and have good communication, critical thinking, math, technical and interpersonal skills.

Certification is not required to work as an aerospace technician, but skills-based programs can help you earn certification through the Federal Aviation Commission, which can increase your hiring potential.

Certificate and diploma programs offered by vocational-technical schools provide training for work as an aerospace technician, but employers increasingly seek candidates with an associate in aerospace engineering technology degree. Aerospace technicians seeking to work on defense contracts must qualify for a security clearance, which sometimes requires U.S. citizenship.

Essential Career Information

Median Pay$61,460

Entry-level education requirements Associate's degree

Aerospace Engineers

An entry-level aerospace engineer may need a bachelor's degree in aerospace engineering or a related field.

Candidates for an aerospace engineer career need analytical and critical thinking skills and the ability to handle complex problem-solving. Many aeronautical engineers work on defense projects for the U.S. government, which requires a security clearance.

Some schools partner with companies to give prospective aerospace engineers practical experience while earning their degree. Some universities also offer five-year programs for candidates to earn both a bachelor's and a master's degree in aeronautical engineering. Advanced education may qualify an aerospace engineer to teach or work in product research and development.

Aerospace engineers who gain experience and want to take on more responsibility must earn a license as a professional engineer, which generally requires a degree from an accredited engineering program and passing scores on the Fundamentals of Engineering and the Professional Engineering exams.

Aeronautical engineers can take the Fundamentals of Engineering exam after earning a bachelor's degree, at which point they serve as engineers-in-training or engineer interns to acquire enough experience to take the Principles and Practice of Engineering exam.

Aerospace engineers in several states must take continuing education courses to maintain their licenses.

Essential Career Information

Median Pay$ 102,420

Entry-level education requirements Bachelor's degree

Maintenance and Repair Careers

Since most items mechanical in nature or which use electricity must be installed, maintenance or repaired, skilled installation, maintenance and repair technicians have plenty of work opportunities.

Maintenance technicians play an important role in the repair and upkeep of equipment, machines and buildings. Their work environment depends on their specialization and employer. Maintenance technicians are also known as machinery maintenance workers, industrial machinery mechanics, and electro-mechanical technicians.

There's an array of installation, maintenance and repair careers to choose from. These careers are available in a variety of settings. Some installation, maintenance, and repair careers require on-the-job training, whereas some of these careers require the completion of a formal training program.

Maintenance and Repair Careers:

- Aircraft and Avionics Equipment Mechanics and Technicians

- Automotive Body and Glass Repairers

- Automotive Service Technicians and Mechanics

- Computer, ATM, and Office Machine Repairers

- Diesel Service Technicians and Mechanics

- Electrical and Electronic Installers and Repairers

- General Maintenance and Repair Workers

- Heating, Air Conditioning and Refrigeration Mechanics and Installers

- Heavy Vehicle and Mobile Equipment Service Technicians

- Home Appliance Repairers

- Industrial Machinery Mechanics and Machinery Maintenance Workers

- Line Installers and Repairers

- Medical Appliance Technicians

- Medical Equipment Repairers

- Millwrights

- Small Engine Mechanics

- Telecommunications Equipment Installers and Repairers

Automotive Body and Glass Repairers

Automotive body and glass repairers restore, refinish, and replace vehicle bodies and frames, windshields, and window glass.

Essential requirement

Education requirement High school diploma or equivalent

Median pay $40,580

Automotive service technicians and mechanics

Automotive service technicians and mechanics, often called service technicians or service techs, inspect, maintain, and repair cars and light trucks.

Essential requirement

Education requirement Postsecondary nondegree award

Median pay $39,550

Management Careers

Skilled managers are in demand in an array of industries. Managers with the appropriate experience and credentials are some of the world's highest paid professionals.

The three basic management levels include top-level manager, middle manager and lower manager. People seeking management careers need skills such as leadership, communication, motivational and interpersonal.

The major industries providing management careers include healthcare facilities, wholesalers, banks, business service companies, government agencies, insurance companies, retail businesses and schools.

Education requirements for management jobs vary by the company or organization. Some employers require a bachelor degree or an associate degree or some post-secondary education. Some management jobs require a Master in Business Administration (MBA) degree or a master degree in another field.

Management Careers:

- Administrative Services Managers

- Advertising, Promotions, and Marketing Managers

- Architectural and Engineering Managers

- Compensation and Benefits Managers

- Computer and Information Systems Managers

- Engineering Managers

- Farmers, Ranchers and Other Agricultural Managers

- Financial Managers

- Food Service Managers

- Human Resources Managers

- Industrial Production Managers

- Legislators

- Lodging Managers

- Management Analysts

- Medical and Health Services Managers

- Natural Sciences Managers

- Post-secondary Education Administrators

- Preschool and Childcare Center Directors

- Property, Real Estate, and Community Association Managers

- Public Relations Managers and Specialists

- Sales Managers

- Social and Community Service Managers

- Top Executives

Administrative Services Managers

Administrative services managers plan, direct, and coordinate supportive services of an organization. Their specific responsibilities vary, but administrative service managers typically maintain facilities and supervise activities that include recordkeeping, mail distribution, and office upkeep.

Essential career information

Education requirement Bachelor's degree

Median pay $94,020

Advertising, Promotions, and Marketing Managers

Advertising, promotions, and marketing managers plan programs to generate interest in products or services. They work with art directors, sales agents, and financial staff members.

Essential career information

Education requirement Bachelor's degree

Median pay $129,380

Architectural and Engineering Managers

Architectural and engineering managers plan, direct, and coordinate activities in architectural and engineering companies.

Essential career information

Education requirement Bachelor's degree

Median pay $137,720

Art and Media

The dynamic world of art and design provides an array of career opportunities from designing floral arrangements to creating movie sets. The range of art and design careers provides opportunities for just about every creative person. Art and design careers such as graphic designer and interior designer combine creativity with practical skills, whereas a fashion designer career relies more on creativity.

Just about every sector needs people with art and design degrees for rewarding niche roles. People with art and design careers use their creative skills to communicate their client's message. The art and design sector can be quite competitive, with technical skills increasingly important for many art and design jobs.

Freelance artists who sell their own artwork benefit from more artistic freedom, flexible scheduling and the ability to select their projects. They must manage their finances, marketing and public relations.

Art Careers:

- Art Directors

- Craft and Fine Artists

- Fashion Designers

- Floral Designers

- Graphic Designers

- Industrial Designers

- Interior Designers

- Jewelers and Precious Stone and Metal Workers

- Multimedia Artists and Animators

- Set and Exhibit Designers

Art Directors

An art director career typically requires a Bachelor of Arts or Bachelor of Fine Arts and three to five years of previous work experience in a related position, such as graphic designer, illustrator, copyeditor, or photographer.

Some colleges and universities offer a Bachelor of Design, a Bachelor of Visual Communications, a Bachelor in Multimedia Design and Development, a Bachelor in Design Management, a Bachelor in Graphic Design, or a Bachelor in Digital Media degree program.

Some art directors hoping to advance in their career continue their education with a Master of Fine Arts (MFA) or Master of Business Administration (MBA) degree.

Art directors don't need a specific license or certification.

Media Careers:

- Announcers

- Art Directors

- Broadcast and Sound Engineering Technicians

- Editors

- Film and Video Editors and Camera Operators

- Graphic Designers

- Interpreters and Translators

- Photographers

- Reporters, Correspondents, and Broadcast News Analysts

- Technical Writers

- Writers and Authors

The media/news/communications industry has an array of rewarding careers for dedicated professionals with good communications skills. The increasingly popular online media provides an array of job opportunities.

Technology provides more opportunities for the media/news/communications industry to offer audio and visual messages to the public.

People seeking a media, news or communications career benefit from gaining experience through an internship or through working for a college newspaper. Some of the careers in the media/news/communications industry require a bachelor degree.

Business and Finance Careers

Business careers are available in just about every industry. People with business skills are in demand in large corporations, small companies, nonprofits and government agencies. Business careers provide viable ways to build long, rewarding careers.

Due to the vast nature of the business world, there are no required set of skills; each career has its unique requirements, some business careers require an aptitude for math, whereas other business careers require excellent communications and interpersonal skills.

Business and Finance careers

- Actuaries

- Accountants and Auditors

- Appraisers and Assessors of Real Estate

- Budget Analysts

- Claims Adjusters, Appraisers, Examiners, and Investigators

- Cost Estimators

- Financial Analysts

- Financial Clerks

- Human Resources Specialists

- Insurance Underwriters

- Loan Officers

- Logisticians

- Management Analysts

- Market Research Analysts

- Meeting, Convention and Events Planners

- Operations Research Analysts

- Personal Financial Advisors

- Purchasing Managers, Buyers and Purchasing Agents

- Statisticians

Accountants and Auditors

Accountants and auditors prepare and examine financial records. They ensure that financial records are accurate and that taxes are paid properly and on time. Accountants and auditors assess financial operations and work to help ensure that organizations run efficiently.

Essential career information

Education requirement Bachelor's degree

Median pay $69,350

Appraisers and Assessors of Real Estate

Appraisers and assessors of real estate provide a value estimate on land and buildings usually before they are sold, mortgaged, taxed, insured, or developed.

Essential career information

Education requirement: Bachelor's degree

2017 median pay $54,010

Budget analysts

Budget analysts help public and private institutions organize their finances. They prepare budget reports and monitor institutional spending.

Essential career information

Education requirement: Bachelor's degree

2017 median pay $75,240

Administrative work

Administrative support employees work in practically every industry. Duties vary by the specific office assistant job and company, however, duties for often assistants typically involve clerical tasks and back-office duties. Many administrative assistant jobs provide opportunities for increases in pay and career advancement.

Administrative Support and Clerical Careers:

- Administrative Services Managers

- Bill and Account Collectors

- Bookkeepers and Accounting and Auditing Clerks

- Cargo and Freight Agents

- Couriers and Messengers

- Customer Service Representatives

- Desktop Publishers

- Financial Clerks

- General Office Clerks

- Information Clerks

- Medical Records and Health Information Technicians

- Paralegals and Legal Assistants

- Secretaries and Administrative Assistants

Community and Social Service

Community and social service occupations include social workers, counselors, and religious workers. Employment of community and social service occupations is projected to grow 14 percent from 2016 to 2026, faster than the average for all occupations, adding about 371,900 jobs. Most projected new jobs in this occupational group are in counselor and social worker occupations, as their services will continue to be needed in areas such as drug abuse counseling and rehabilitation counseling, and for school and career counseling.

The median annual wage for community and social service occupations was $43,840 in May 2017, which was higher than the median annual wage for all occupations of $37,690.

Social and Human Service Assistants

Social and human service assistants provide client services, including support for families, in a wide variety of fields, such as psychology, rehabilitation, and social work. They assist other workers, such as social workers, and they help clients find benefits or community services.

Essential career information:

Entry level education: High school diploma or equivalent

2017 median pay $33,120

(source: Bureau of labor statistics)

Rehabilitation Counselors

Rehabilitation counselors help people with physical, mental, developmental, or emotional disabilities live independently. They work with clients to overcome or manage the personal, social, or psychological effects of disabilities on employment or independent living.

Essential career information

Entry requirement: Master's degree

2017 median pay $34,860

(source: Bureau of labor statistics)

Substance abuse and behavioral disorder counselors

Substance abuse, behavioral disorder, and mental health counselors advise people who suffer from alcoholism, drug addiction, eating disorders, mental health issues, or other mental or behavioral problems. They provide treatment and support to help clients recover from addiction or modify problem behaviors. Median pay $43,300

Health educators

Health educators teach people about behaviors that promote wellness. They develop and implement strategies to improve the health of individuals and communities. Community health workers collect data and discuss health concerns with members of specific populations or communities.

Median pay $45,360

Social Workers

Social workers help people solve and cope with problems in their everyday lives. Clinical social workers also diagnose and treat mental, behavioral, and emotional issues.

Median pay $47,980

Mental health counselors and marriage and family therapists

Marriage and family therapists help people manage and overcome problems with family and other relationships.

Essential information

Entry requirement Master's degree

Median pay $48,790

(source: Bureau of labor statistics)

Probation officers and correctional treatment specialists

Probation officers and correctional treatment specialists provide social services to assist in rehabilitation of law offenders in custody or on probation or parole.

Essential career information

Entry requirement Bachelor's degree

Median pay $51,410

School and Career Counselors

School counselors help students develop the academic and social skills needed to succeed in school. Career counselors help people choose careers and follow a path to employment.

Entry requirement to the profession is master's degree, and the median pay is $55,410

Education Careers

The education sector provides rewarding education careers such as elementary school teacher and special education teacher. The education field offers careers besides teaching careers such as instructional coordinator, archivist and librarian. A lot of the education careers require postsecondary education and strong interpersonal skills.

Every state requires schoolteachers to have certification. State education boards provide certification to teachers for specific grade levels or specific subjects. Teachers need to have a bachelor's degree and complete a training program, including student teaching. Sometimes specialty teachers need to have a master's degree.

Education Careers:

- Adult Literacy & GED Teachers

- Archivists

- Career Teachers & Technical Education Teachers

- Curators, Museum Technicians & Conservators

- Health Educators

- High School Teachers

- Instructional Coordinators

- Kindergarten & Elementary School Teachers

- Librarians

- Library Technicians & Assistants

- Middle School Teachers

- Post-Secondary Education Administrators

- Postsecondary Teachers

- Preschool & Childcare Center Directors

- Preschool Teachers

- School & Career Counselors

- Self-Enrichment Teachers

- Special Education Teachers

- Teacher Assistants

Legal Occupations

Employment of legal occupations is projected to grow 9 percent from 2016 to 2026, about as fast as the average for all occupations, which will result in about 116,200 new jobs. As law firms try to increase the efficiency of legal services and reduce their costs, there is expected to be strong demand to hire many more paralegals and legal assistants. Additionally, the demand for lawyers is expected to continue as individuals, businesses, and governments require legal services in many areas.

The median annual wage for legal occupations was $80,080 in May 2017, which was higher than the median annual wage for all occupations of $37,690.

Arbitrators, Mediators, and Conciliators

Arbitrators, mediators, and conciliators facilitate negotiation and dialogue between disputing parties to help resolve conflicts outside of the court system.

Entry requirement: Bachelor's degree

2017 Median pay $60,670

Court reporters

Court reporters create word-for-word transcriptions at trials, depositions, and other legal proceedings. Some court reporters provide captioning for television and real-time translation for deaf or hard-of-hearing people at public events, in business meetings, or classrooms.

Entry requirement: Postsecondary Nano degree award

2017 median pay $55,120

Judges, mediators, and hearing officers

Judges and hearing officers apply the law by overseeing the legal process in courts. They also conduct pretrial hearings, resolve administrative disputes, facilitate negotiations between opposing parties, and issue legal decisions.

Entry requirement: Doctoral or professional degree

2017 median pay $115,520

Lawyers

Lawyers advise and represent individuals, businesses, and government agencies on legal issues and disputes.

Entry requirement: Doctoral or professional degree

2017 median pay $119,250

Paralegals and legal assistants

Paralegals and legal assistants perform a variety of tasks to support lawyers, including maintaining and organizing files, conducting legal research, and drafting documents.

Entry requirement Associate's degree

2017 median pay $50,410

Protective Service

Employment of protective service occupations is projected to grow 5 percent from 2016 to 2026, about as fast as the average for all occupations, which will result in about 158,200 new jobs.

Protective service occupations had a median annual wage of $39,550 in May 2017, which was slightly higher than the median annual wage for all occupations of $37,690.

Correctional officers and Bailiffs

Correctional officers are responsible for overseeing individuals who have been arrested and are awaiting trial or who have been sentenced to serve time in jail or prison. Bailiffs are law enforcement officers who maintain safety and order in courtrooms.

Entry requirements: High school diploma or equivalent

2017 median pay $43,510

Fire inspectors and investigators

Fire inspectors examine buildings in order to detect fire hazards and ensure that federal, state, and local fire codes are met. Fire investigators, another type of worker in this field, determine the origin and cause of fires and explosions. Forest fire inspectors and prevention specialists assess outdoor fire hazards in public and residential areas.

2017 median pay $56,670

Firefighters

Firefighters control and put out fires and respond to emergencies where life, property, or the environment is at risk.

Education requirement Postsecondary nondegree award

2017 median pay $49,080

Police and Detectives

Police officers protect lives and property. Detectives and criminal investigators, who are sometimes called agents or special agents, gather facts and collect evidence of possible crimes.

2017 median pay $62,960

Private Detectives and Investigators

Private detectives and investigators search for information about legal, financial, and personal matters. They offer many services, such as verifying people's backgrounds and statements, finding missing persons, and investigating computer crimes.

Education requirement: High school diploma or equivalent
2017 median pay $50,700

Security Guards and Gaming Surveillance Officers

Security guards and gaming surveillance officers patrol and protect property against theft, vandalism, and other illegal activity.

Education requirement: High school diploma or equivalent
2017 median pay $26,960

CULTURE SHOCK AND ITS EFFECTS

1. The Honeymoon Stage

This happened to me when I first Landed in Detroit, Michigan and later in a smaller airport in Vermont. The whole experience was exciting, and my hotel room was something out of this world, I loved each moment. Remember that on short trips, the honeymoon phase may take over the entire experience as the later effects of culture shock don't have time to set in. However, on longer trips, the honeymoon stage will usually phase out eventually.

2. The Frustration Stage

During the frustration stage, I had to learn more about transportation. Taking the bus was the worst experience, especially during the winter and snow. It was a frustrating experience because I did not know how to drive. Don't be like me! Come to America equipped with driving skills. Public transportation in the United States is not dependable; therefore, be ready to drive your own personal car. Therefore, do not give up, focus on why you immigrated to the United States because eventually, things will get better. People have done it and you can survive culture shock too. My general advice is do not compare America to your home country, instead learn how to adapt because America is not the issue, believe me, the issue is that you must accept changes and adapt to your new country.

3. The Adjustment Stage

I finally accepted and enjoyed America. In America, I have learnt to maintain eye contact a sign of genuine and honest conversation. Avoid crossing arms, which can be a sign of loss of interest in the conversation. A smile will go a long way to make others feel good. Every culture has its unspoken rules that govern how people interact with and treat one another. I hope you enjoyed this book; the information will cut your learning curve in the United States. I wish you success in your career ambitions.

www.ingramcontent.com/pod-product-compliance
Lightning Source LLC
Chambersburg PA
CBHW021222090426
42740CB00006B/337